# The Interferon Crusade

SANDRA PANEM

# The Interferon Crusade

THE BROOKINGS INSTITUTION
*Washington, D.C.*

*Copyright © 1984 by*
THE BROOKINGS INSTITUTION
*1775 Massachusetts Avenue, N.W., Washington, D.C. 20036*

*Library of Congress Cataloging in Publication data:*

Panem, Sandra, 1946–
  The interferon crusade.
  Includes index.
  1. Interferon—Research—History.   I. Title.
QR187.5.P36   1984     616.99′4061     84-17629
ISBN 0-8157-6900-9
ISBN 0-8157-6899-0 (pbk.)


1 2 3 4 5 6 7 8 9

THE BROOKINGS INSTITUTION is an independent organization devoted to nonpartisan research, education, and publication in economics, government, foreign policy, and the social sciences generally. Its principal purposes are to aid in the development of sound public policies and to promote public understanding of issues of national importance.

The Institution was founded on December 8, 1927, to merge the activities of the Institute for Government Research, founded in 1916, the Institute of Economics, founded in 1922, and the Robert Brookings Graduate School of Economics and Government, founded in 1924.

The Board of Trustees is responsible for the general administration of the Institution, while the immediate direction of the policies, program, and staff is vested in the President, assisted by an advisory committee of the officers and staff. The by-laws of the Institution state: "It is the function of the Trustees to make possible the conduct of scientific research, and publication, under the most favorable conditions, and to safeguard the independence of the research staff in the pursuit of their studies and in the publication of the results of such studies. It is not a part of their function to determine, control, or influence the conduct of particular investigations or the conclusions reached."

The President bears final responsibility for the decision to publish a manuscript as a Brookings book. In reaching his judgment on the competence, accuracy, and objectivity of each study, the President is advised by the director of the appropriate research program and weighs the views of a panel of expert outside readers who report to him in confidence on the quality of the work. Publication of a work signifies that it is deemed a competent treatment worthy of public consideration but does not imply endorsement of conclusions or recommendations.

The Institution maintains its position of neutrality on issues of public policy in order to safeguard the intellectual freedom of the staff. Hence interpretations or conclusions in Brookings publications should be understood to be solely those of the authors and should not be attributed to the Institution, to its trustees, officers, or other staff members, or to the organizations that support its research.

# Foreword

In the mid-1970s a series of technical innovations revolutionized biomedical research, with profound implications for research and development in the agricultural, petrochemical, pharmaceutical, and chemical industries. Because of the technology's economic promise and its potential hazards, congressional committees, the Office of Technology Assessment, and the White House have recently convened groups to examine the U.S. position on biotechnology. Comparable actions by the Organization for Economic Cooperation and Development and the Japanese Ministry of International Trade and Industry confirm the widespread interest in these developments.

In this book Sandra Panem traces the development of interferon to highlight the policy issues raised by the biotechnology revolution. She describes the scientific and political events that shaped the crusade to research and develop interferon. She then discusses the public policy questions that face the biomedical profession concerning the relations between the federal government, industry, and academe in the areas of basic research, technology transfer, and the development of new commercial products and markets. She argues for renewed federal commitment to support fundamental biomedical research, and suggests that scientists become more actively involved in the political process of setting the federal research agenda.

Sandra Panem was a science and public policy fellow in the Brookings Economic Studies program during 1982–83. She is grateful to Joy Robinson for her research assistance; to Jan Vilček, Robert Morgan, Victoria Schauf, and Christine M. Helms for their encouragement and criticism; and to Alice M. Rivlin, Louise B. Russell, Paul Ginsburg, Harriet Zuckerman, Marilyn Bach, and Hans Weill for their helpful comments on the manuscript. Many colleagues in the interferon field shared their experiences, in particular Maureen W. Meyers and George J. Galasso. Susan L. Woollen provided editorial, research, and secretarial assistance; Molly B. C. Ruzicka edited the manuscript; Penelope

Schmitt and Carolyn A. Rutsch verified its factual content; Bonnie Urciolli transcribed the interviews; and Ward & Silvan prepared the index.

During her work on this book, Panem was supported by grants from the Alfred P. Sloan Foundation and the W. K. Kellogg Foundation. Budgetary data were provided by the National Institutes of Health and the National Institute of Allergy and Infectious Diseases. Part of the second chapter draws on a December 1982 article in the *Atlantic Monthly* by Sandra Panem and Jan Vilček. Part of the fourth chapter appeared in the Winter 1982 issue of the *Brookings Review*.

The views in this book are those of the author and should not be ascribed to the persons or organizations whose assistance is acknowledged or to the trustees, officers, or other staff members of the Brookings Institution.

BRUCE K. MACLAURY
*President*

*August 1984*
*Washington, D.C.*

# Contents

## Figures

*Chapter One*

# Introduction

In 1964, seven years after the discovery of interferon, the first international meeting of interferon scientists was held in Bratislava, Czechoslovakia. The meeting's 40-odd participants included virtually everyone working in the field. In contrast, in 1982 three international meetings, each attracting 300 to 400 persons, were devoted wholly to interferon. Interferon also figured prominently that year on the meeting agendas of professional scientific and medical organizations. Although there are no documented figures on the number of U.S. scientists who were actively engaged in interferon research and development in 1982, 1,000 would be a conservative estimate. The explosion of interest in interferon that these recent figures reflect testifies to the success of a crusade to research and develop interferon. This book is concerned with the scientific and political events that shaped that undertaking and with the policy issues involved in mobilizing biomedical research.

## Interferon's History and Development

Several stories are interwoven in the history of the interferon crusade, beginning with the discovery of interferon in England in 1957 by Alick Isaacs and Jean Lindenmann. Isaacs and Lindenmann observed that cells produce a natural protein that "interferes" with virus infections (hence the name *interferon*).[1] Originally thought to be a single substance, the interferons are now known to be a family of proteins that differ significantly from one another in chemical structure and biological

1. For a detailed review of the technological and scientific history of interferon, the reader is referred to several general works: Robert M. Friedman, *Interferons: A Primer* (New York: Academic Press, 1981); William E. Stewart II, *The Interferon System*, 2d ed. (Vienna and New York: Springer-Verlag, 1981); and *Interferon*, a series of annual volumes edited by Ion Gresser (Academic Press, 1979–).

1

functions.[2] Moreover, the first recognized effect of interferon—to help the body fight virus infections—has now been shown to be only one of its functions. Interferons form a complicated system of potent hormone-like substances[3] that are involved in the regulation of immunity and possibly also in embryonic development, growth regulation, and nerve function. In addition, interferon is being evaluated extensively as a drug for treatment of cancer.

The lure of interferon as a cancer cure and the resulting mobilization of many astute scientists and politicians in pursuit of such a cure is the second story in the history of the interferon experience. Convinced that interferon's potential to combat cancer should not go undeveloped, private citizens, medical foundations, members of Congress, and vocal scientists focused political and media attention on interferon during the late 1970s and early 1980s. This interest culminated in the marshaling of substantial resources toward researching and clinically testing interferon as an antitumor drug. So successful was this effort to target research that industry invested heavily in interferon's development.

The third story in the interferon experience involves interferon's role in the mid-1970s as the focus of an emerging biotechnology industry, based on a technical revolution known popularly as genetic engineering. Many companies interested in the new technology that allows isolating and splicing together portions of genetic material chose interferon as their demonstration project. Genetic engineering not only makes most biological problems more amenable to study but often does away with previous research constraints, such as limited supplies of starting materials for extraction of biological substances, and expensive and difficult procedures that resulted in limited amounts of impure substances. The solution to an increasing number of biomedical problems is now reduced to selecting projects for study and allocating relevant resources (such as personnel, funds, and instrumentation).

Throughout this book, reference is made to a "traditional" scheme

2. Interferons made by human cells are now referred to as alpha, beta, and gamma interferons based on the nucleic acid sequences of the genes that direct their synthesis. As of summer 1983, twenty distinct interferons have been identified in man. Full descriptions of these interferons are found in the references cited in footnote 1 and in Maureen W. Myers, "Interferon Nomenclature," *ASM News*, vol. 50, no. 2 (1984), pp. 68–69.

3. Hormones can be defined as chemicals that are produced by cells and that are secreted into the blood and act on other cells to regulate specific biological functions, for example, insulin and estrogens.

of doing research, which is what occurred between the late 1950s and the late 1970s, before genetic engineering. Then, university-based work was generously subsidized through government funds, and the scientific ethos was that an academic researcher was limited only by his or her intellectual ingenuity. A research program judged as sound by scientific peers could be confident of federal government support. The peer review system was generally perceived to foster independent and honest scientific oversight. Moreover, professional stature was achieved by thorough, rapid, and open dissemination of new findings and ideas. The advent of genetic engineering with its extraordinary commercial opportunities for biologists, along with increasing competition for federal research support, significantly changed the research environment.

## Reasons for Studying the Interferon Experience

In addition to chronicling the history of interferon, this book uses interferon as a case study to analyze policy issues on the choice and pursuit of biomedical research within the context of a technical revolution. In this regard, the unique events of the interferon experience provide eight reasons for its study.

First, interferon research itself has been radically altered as a result of genetic engineering. Until 1982–83 the main obstacle to progress in research was the lack of "pure" interferon in sufficient quantity at a reasonable cost. Genetic engineering technology has now overcome these constraints.

The second reason to examine interferon relates to the fact that numerous commercial concerns independently chose interferon to test their early biotechnology efforts. The biotechnology industry today consists of two classes of corporations. One class is composed of small genetic engineering companies, many of which were founded in the late 1970s to capitalize on the new technology. The other class comprises the large pharmaceutical and chemical corporations that have traditionally been engaged in producing biologicals and that expanded their research and development (R&D) to include the new biotechnology. For the small "genetic boutiques" the gamble was twofold—that they could employ the technology to produce a product and that interferon would be medically useful. In addition, these companies were dependent on interferon's commercial success; for some, interferon was to be their first product. For large drug houses (such as Schering-Plough Corporation, Hoffmann-La Roche, G. D. Searle and Company, and the Wellcome Research Laboratories), the main risk was whether interferon could be produced quickly enough to make their particular firm the leader in the interferon market. And, like the smaller concerns, they were wagering that interferon would be needed and used by the medical community. The reasoning behind a company's decision to choose interferon as a biotechnology demonstration project (Eli Lilly and Company, for example, selected insulin rather than interferon as its first genetically engineered product) provides public policy observers with an excellent opportunity to evaluate the role of extrascientific factors such as media hype and political lobbying in setting biomedical research priorities.

A third reason for studying the interferon experience is that it demonstrates a range of policy issues that are raised by an emerging industry. Although some of these issues are not new to the biomedical community, they now have increasing urgency. The extensive new opportunities to commercialize academic research findings can easily lead to conflicts of interest. The academic community is facing some hard questions. What should be the guidelines for university faculty as entrepreneurs? Should faculty hold management positions? Can fundamental research done as an academic scientist be distinguished from applied research done as an entrepreneur? Should the professor-entrepreneur be permitted to perform work of related content in both spheres? How do universities, their faculties, and their government and industry sponsors arrange ownership rights? Should universities go into business with their faculties? These questions, which had not much troubled the biomedical academic community in the past, became pressing issues in the interferon experience.

A fourth reason to study interferon relates to the conflict-of-interest questions just posed and involves the way in which the interferon experience exemplifies new patterns in the exchange of scientific information. Secrecy in research becomes a central concern when proprietary interests are juxtaposed with traditional academic values. Several questions are raised in this regard. Is secrecy an inevitable consequence when an esoteric area of basic research matures into a field ready for commercial development? Has a quantitative or qualitative change in research secrecy occurred as commercial biotechnology has grown? Is there a difference between secrecy imposed by individual choice and that imposed by contractual agreement? Is the cost of having to submit experimental findings to an industrial sponsor prior to making the data public an excessive price for the academic scientist to pay for long-term and generous commercial support? Does the assessment of cost depend on the time delay between submission and public announcement of findings, which could be anywhere from one month to several years? Is the trade-off for the individual scientist the same as that for the general scientific community and for the general public, who are the ultimate consumers of science? Attempts to answer these and other questions on the secrecy issue serve to underscore the changes that have occurred in biomedical research and development since the introduction of genetic engineering.

By way of explanation, scientific discovery and its technological application can be divided into three distinct phases. Phase one includes events that lead to the discovery of a phenomenon, its description, and its mechanistic explanation. Before genetic engineering, phase-one work was done either at universities, in research institutes, or, occasionally, in industrial research institutes.

Phase two is a period of application, in which processes are developed to exploit phenomena discovered in phase one (for instance, purification of interferon and large-scale fermentation of bacteria to produce more interferon by organisms carrying interferon genes). In this transitional stage, before genetic engineering, work was done predominantly in the commercial sector and in academic settings in which process development was the research subject (for example, schools of agriculture and departments of applied microbiology).

Phase three is a developmental period in which work is confined to manufacturing, packaging, and marketing the products derived from phases one and two. Clinical trials and collection of data to fulfill federal requirements for drug approval are also performed during this stage. Phase-three work has occurred and continues to occur within the private sector.[4]

Before the late 1970s, the three stages were separated both by the work site (academe versus private industry) and in time. It was not unusual for the time lag between initial discovery of a phenomenon, its translation into a process or product, and the appearance of a product in the marketplace to be several decades or more. This time factor is in

4. Although phase-three work takes place in the private sector, industry often contracted for clinical trials that were performed in academic medical centers.

large part responsible for the academic community's perception that fundamental research is both different in content and displaced from applied research and development.

With genetic engineering came a tremendous change in the way biomedical research proceeded—a change that can be viewed as a "time collapse." For example, whereas it took thirty-two years to complete phase-one through phase-three work on the first pacemaker,[5] the fundamental experiments with recombinant-DNA techniques were performed between 1971 and 1973;[6] the first insulin gene was cloned in 1977;[7] and the first genetically engineered insulin[8] was approved for sale by the Food and Drug Administration (FDA) in late 1982. Less than nine years elapsed, therefore, between phase one and the completion of phase three, including the time-consuming clinical trials for testing insulin. As phase-one work moves increasingly into the private sector, the issues of secrecy and information exchange are highlighted, owing to time collapse.

A fifth reason to examine the interferon experience is that it exposes a number of manpower problems, both in academe and in industry. Given the financial pull of private industry, the ability of universities to recruit and retain high-quality faculties is a growing concern. Similarly, industrial requirements for technically sophisticated workers have been altered, raising the possibility that the manpower needs of biotechnology may emerge as a serious problem in the next decade.

The sixth reason for studying interferon involves a number of ethical concerns related to the conflict-of-interest concerns mentioned earlier. Foremost among these are the relationships between the student and the professor-entrepreneur, and between the professor-entrepreneur and the institution-corporation. Should a professor's entrepreneurial rela-

5. Battelle Memorial Institute, Columbus Laboratories, *Final Report on Analysis of Selected Biomedical Research Programs to President's Biomedical Research Panel, January 31, 1976,* vol. 1 (Columbus, Ohio: Battelle, 1976), pp. 25–26.

6. The fundamental findings were the discoveries of reverse transcriptase and restriction enzymes. See David Baltimore, "Viruses, Polymerases and Cancer," text of lecture on receipt of the Nobel Prize in physiology and medicine, *Science,* vol. 192 (May 14, 1976), pp. 632–36. See also Hamilton O. Smith, "Nucleotide Sequence Specificity of Restriction Endonucleases: Nobel Lecture, December 8, 1978," *Science,* vol. 205 (August 3, 1979), pp. 455–62.

7. Axel Ullrich and others, "Rat Insulin Genes: Construction of Plasmids Containing the Coding Sequences," *Science,* vol. 196 (June 17, 1977), pp. 1313–19.

8. Human insulin produced by genetic engineering techniques by Eli Lilly and Company is known as Humulin.

tions be disclosed? If so, how and to what extent? Should students participate in commercially oriented work? Should students and post-doctoral trainees be offered monetary incentives for their work? Although this study deals only tangentially with the legal and ethical questions that have been raised in biotechnology in connection with the development of interferon, the importance of these dilemmas should not be discounted.

The seventh reason why interferon makes a good case study is that it provides a model of how research can be effectively supported by the public and private sectors. From World War II until 1974, an increasing amount of university-based biomedical research was funded by the federal government.[9] By 1974 institutions granting doctoral and master's degrees in the biological and medical sciences derived 74.2 percent of their research and development budgets from the federal government. This percentage remained stable through 1981.[10]

In the current period of declining federal resources for biomedical research, the debate on how to spend federal research funds has intensified. Grants represent a mechanism by which the individual researcher solicits government funds for a project he or she wishes to conduct. In contrast, the government solicits proposals from researchers by announcing that contracts are available for specific work. The federal government has extensively used both grant and contract funding to stimulate development of interferon. Industry has also been actively involved in this field, and examples of parallel private and public support of interferon basic research occur. The interaction of commercial and noncommercial research efforts, as well as government support for industrial efforts, can be examined in the interferon example.

The eighth and final reason to examine this case is that interferon research exemplifies the problems that occur when the rate of information generated expands dramatically. For example, can the policies for licensing drugs and issuing patents handle the increased volume of applications? And what will determine the number of interferon variants that will be manufactured?

9. A detailed discussion of the growth of the federal biomedical research budget is found in Stephen P. Strickland, *Politics, Science, and Dread Disease: A Short History of United States Medical Research Policy* (Harvard University Press, 1972).

10. National Science Foundation, *Academic Science/Engineering R&D Funds, Fiscal Year 1981*, Surveys of Science Resources Series NSF 83-308 (Washington, D.C.: NSF, 1983), tables B3, B4.

## Information Sources

Information in this book is derived from three sources. The first is extensive interviews by the author with scientists who have worked with interferon in the public, private, or academic sectors; with people who have allocated resources for interferon research; and with people who were instrumental in promoting interest in interferon. Many subjects were interviewed more than once; some of them requested anonymity. Informal conversations were also held with numerous other people connected with interferon.

The second source is computerized data from the National Institutes of Health (NIH) on resource allocations for interferon as well as other areas of biomedical research. The third source is secondary references, such as journals, newspapers, books, and computerized lists of publications.

These sources helped to illuminate the development of interferon research, the technological breakthroughs in other biomedical fields that affected interferon research, and the people, political events, and historical accidents that have figured prominently in the interferon effort.

Understanding the interferon experience may prove useful in predicting future problems of biomedical research and may serve also as a reference for formulating research policy. An important aspect of this case study to keep in mind is that issues arising during the development of interferon reflect problems that will probably confront most if not all biomedical research in the 1980s as genetic engineering technology is broadly applied. In addition, concerns similar to those resulting from the commercial value of biological research will most likely occur in other scientific areas as they experience technical revolutions.

As Dr. Timothy O'Connor, one of the scientists interviewed for this book, remarked about the revolutionary nature of the interferon experience for biomedicine, "What we're really talking of is the future. Interferon is like the Lindbergh flight to Paris. It demonstrates a principle."

*Chapter Two*

# The Interferon Experience

This chapter outlines the history of interferon from its discovery in 1957 to its extensive use in clinical trials with cancer patients in 1983. Emphasis is placed on defining why interferon engendered the enthusiasm of scientists, politicians, lay-science groups, and venture capitalists in the mid-1970s. Discussion explores the ways in which an evolving scientific data base on interferon affected the scientific and lay communities' view of interferon. Throughout, the attraction of interferon as a potential anticancer agent is stressed. Finally, the costs and benefits of the interferon crusade are assessed in light of the 1983 consensus of scientists that interferon by itself is not likely to replace or even match other, already available forms of cancer treatment.

## Interferon before Genetic Engineering: 1957–78

More than half the infectious diseases that an average person contracts in a lifetime are due to viruses. Virology—the branch of microbiology devoted to the study of viruses—developed from an interest in infectious diseases. First recognized in the nineteenth century as a distinct group of infectious agents mediating transmissible disease, viruses had, until the middle 1950s, been studied in the naturalist's tradition. Typically, extracts were prepared from tissues of diseased animals, were passed through fine-pored porcelain filters (because viruses are so much smaller than other disease-causing microbes, viruses once were defined as "ultrafilterable" agents), and were then introduced into healthy animals, which were observed until they developed disease. The modern biologist's techniques—chemical analysis, X-ray diffraction, biophysical characterization—were difficult to use because viruses could not be produced in sufficient quantity and purity for analysis. Only in the late 1950s did animal virology (the study of viruses in animals and man) emerge as a modern science.

The technological breakthrough that made viruses amenable to modern biochemical study was the development of methods for cell culture, which enabled animal cells to be grown in the laboratory. Viruses are obligate intracellular parasites; in other words, they require a living cell in order to grow. Given the ability to culture cells in the laboratory, viruses could therefore be grown in their host cells. The American microbiologist John F. Enders demonstrated the importance of this technique for virology by applying it to the propagation of poliovirus in the laboratory. For this work, which ushered in modern virology, he (with Thomas H. Weller and Frederick C. Robbins) shared the Nobel prize in physiology and medicine in 1954.

### Discovery of the Interferon Phenomenon

In the 1950s virologists focused their attention on methods to prevent or intercede in viral infection. In his laboratory in Mill Hill, England, on the outskirts of London, Alick Isaacs was studying the growth of influenza virus in chick embryo cells. In 1957 he and a visiting Swiss scientist, Jean Lindenmann, observed that cells exposed to heated influenza viruses became resistant to subsequent influenza infection. When the fluid bathing the surviving cells was added to other cells, the recipients also became resistant to infection. Isaacs realized that the fluids contained a factor that interfered with virus infection, and he named the substance interferon.

A similar phenomenon was observed independently somewhat later in Enders's laboratory at Harvard University. Eduoard De Maeyer, at that time a visiting Belgian postdoctoral fellow working with Enders, recalled the circumstances of these studies:

> Enders and another postdoc, Monto Ho, were working on virus inhibitory factor, VIF, a substance obtained from poliovirus-infected cells, which inhibited the growth of other poliovirus strains. I asked if measles virus would also induce VIF and found something which protected cells—and that was very impressive. After a year or so we had a visit from Alick Isaacs, who was invited to lecture at Harvard. We all went and discovered that we had been working with interferon without knowing that we should call it interferon.[1]

---

1. Information concerning this and all subsequent quotations from interviews is included in the appendix. Quotations not cited by footnotes may be assumed to be from interviews with the author. If a quotation is unaccompanied by a person's name, the source may be assumed to have requested anonymity.

The period of independent confirmation of the interferon phenomenon continued into the early 1960s. Pockets of active interest developed around biomedical scientists such as Charles Chany in France, Pieter De Somer and De Maeyer in Belgium, Kari Cantell in Scandinavia, and Jan Vilček in Czechoslovakia. Later, interest developed in the United States around Samuel Baron, Robert R. Wagner, Maurice R. Hilleman, and Kurt Paucker.

The first formal gathering of the fledgling interferon community occurred in Bratislava, Czechoslovakia, in 1964, an assembly that laid the foundation for a loosely organized international group of interferon enthusiasts.[2] However, despite the excitement that had accompanied its discovery, interferon eluded physical isolation and rigorous chemical definition. Outside the interferon fraternity, interferon was known as a material that resisted chemical characterization, and interferonologists were viewed disparagingly by the scientific establishment as phenomenologists and practitioners of fringe science. One scientist who has worked with interferon since the early 1960s noted that "Isaacs was considered to be a serious virologist who'd become a crackpot, and the scientific community dubbed his discovery 'imaginon.' " Interferon's low image in the mid-1960s can be ascribed to technological limitations. Although interferon research was based on the examination of a compelling biological phenomenon, the lack of appropriate methods for its study led to a virtual stagnation in the field.

For those who remained in the interferon fraternity, a major research problem from 1965 onward was to produce interferon in adequate quantities. Interferon is made by cells in response to viral infection. Complicating the production of interferon is that infected cells manufacture interferon in minute quantities and for only a short time. In addition, it was believed that the only interferon that would be effective in man was the type made in human cells—and only limited supplies of human cells could be grown in the laboratory. Another problem was that of purifying the interferon once it was produced. Not until the late 1970s

2. The first effort to institutionalize this association did not occur until 1983, with the formation of the International Society of Interferon Research, initiated by the American interferonologist William E. Stewart II. The society had its first meeting during the Second TNO Meeting on the biology of the interferon system, in Rotterdam, Netherlands, April 18–22, 1983. (The TNO is the Netherlands' Organization for Applied Scientific Research, established in 1932.) Following a heated discussion, the society elected a committee to examine bylaws and to participate in planning meetings and an interferon journal.

was an important new technological advancement, high-pressure liquid chromatography, applied to the purification of interferon. But the ability to produce enough interferon would remain a limitation until the 1980s.

During the 1960s, interest in interferon centered on its antiviral properties. When the National Institutes of Health, through its National Institute of Allergy and Infectious Diseases (NIAID), formally established an antiviral substances program in 1969, it was with the understanding that interferon would be its cornerstone.[3] In view of the prevailing skepticism about interferon's efficacy, the NIAID program focused first on methods to make and purify interferon. At the same time, pioneering studies in France presaged the changing perception of interferon from that of an antiviral agent to an anticancer agent and, eventually, a hormone that regulates the immune system.

### Interferon Emerges as an Anticancer Agent

The idea that interferon might be useful in treating cancer can be traced to the belief that viruses are the probable cause of many tumors. This idea has been debated since experiments performed in the first decade of this century showed that some forms of cancer in fowl and other animals are caused by viruses. As of 1983, there was still no indisputable proof of a virus causing a human cancer, even though several viral isolates are under intensive investigation. Nevertheless, in the early days of interferon research it was reasoned that if viruses cause cancer, then interferon might prevent or cure cancer through its antiviral activity.

In the late 1960s Dr. Ion Gresser, an American physician and virologist trained in John Enders's laboratory, was working at the Institut de Recherches Scientifiques sur le Cancer in Villejuif, outside Paris. Gresser tried to alter the course of virus-caused leukemias in mice by interferon therapy. His experiments successfully showed that virus-induced cancers could be prevented or delayed by treating animals with interferon. Gresser than tested whether interferon influenced the growth of other mouse tumors that were not likely to be caused by viruses. Following injection of tumor cells into specially bred mouse strains, new tumors formed. To Gresser's surprise, the growth of some of these tumors was delayed by treatment with large doses of interferon.

3. See discussion in chapter 3.

Gresser told a revealing story about the first demonstration of interferon's antitumor activity:

In the fall of 1967, we did an experiment where we injected a transplantable tumor [tumor produced by the injection of cancer cells] into mice. We treated half of the mice with interferon. When the interferon-treated mice had no tumors, but the controls did, I told the technician that there obviously was a mistake, because we did the experiment to show there would be no effect on the growth of the tumor not caused by a virus, and, therefore, interferon really was acting as an antiviral. I told the technician, "You forgot to inject the tumor into this group," and she said, "I injected it," and I said, "No." It stayed that way for a few months until I realized that I had never really answered the question, because I wouldn't accept the results. I repeated the experiment and I injected the tumor. And then it was obvious that interferon had inhibited the growth of the tumor.

At first it was unclear why interferon had inhibited the growth of such transplantable tumors. Now it is known that interferon influences many biological processes. Gresser's experimental work was the first demonstration of interferon's ability to influence immune reactions that, in turn, control susceptibility to infections and can also affect resistance to the growth of cancer cells.

Gresser's findings were not immediately acclaimed by the scientific community. In retrospect, several explanations may be seen to account for the reserved reaction. First, interferon was not unique in causing a modest inhibition of some cancers in mice. Other natural substances and artificially synthesized compounds were also known to cause a similar or greater inhibition of tumor growth in animals. Moreover, many treatments found effective in mice for one reason or another had proved disappointing when applied to human cancer. A more important consideration was the lack of sufficient quantities of human interferon. Since an average human being weighs about 350 times more than a typical laboratory-bred mouse, it was assumed that the amounts of interferon necessary for human use would have to be scaled up accordingly. At the time, technical and economic constraints made it almost unthinkable that enough interferon could be produced to treat a single patient in amounts comparable to the doses given Gresser's mice.

To solve the problem of limited interferon supply, the NIH spurred federal funding of research in the United States for the express purpose of finding ways to increase interferon production (see chapter 3). But at least as important as U.S.-sponsored research was the heroic effort of Kari Cantell in Finland to expand interferon production.

Dr. Cantell developed a facility for the production of human interferon at the government-run Public Health Laboratories in Helsinki. Fresh human blood cells collected in local blood banks were brought to the central laboratory and infected with virus. Interferon induced in these human cells was then painstakingly isolated by a complex purification procedure. Cantell's main contribution was the development of practical methods for the production and partial purification of interferon. Yet the material produced by Cantell, the most potent then available, was only 0.01 percent to 0.10 percent interferon.

Cantell's effort was supported in part by both the Finnish Red Cross and the NIAID. George J. Galasso, who headed the NIAID's Development and Applications Branch (DAB), commented: "We have had a hand in supporting interferon research done abroad because we bought interferon from the Finnish Red Cross and Kari Cantell—I imagine we were his first big customer. The profit the Finnish Red Cross made enabled Cantell to collaborate with other investigators. Cantell could provide interferon for clinical trials, such as in his collaboration with Hans Strander."

### Hans Strander and Osteogenic Sarcoma

General interest in the interferon produced by Cantell was enhanced by preliminary tests of clinical efficacy conducted in the early 1970s by Dr. Hans Strander, a Swedish physician at the Karolinska Institute in Stockholm. As an extrapolation of Gresser's experiments in mice,[4] Strander wanted to determine whether interferon might be useful in antitumor therapy in humans. Strander's preliminary experiments with interferon treatment of human osteogenic sarcoma (a rare but extremely malignant bone cancer) were pivotal in focusing interest on interferon. In fact, his work received media attention to a degree unwarranted by its level of scientific certainty. A New York Times editorial, entitled "New Forms of Therapy," said:

Another new therapeutic modality is interferon, the antiviral chemical pro-

---

4. In an October 1981 interview with the author, Strander said that Gresser's experiments were the most important part of his decision to experiment with interferon, especially because Strander's mentor, Cantell, had collaborated in the early 1960s with Kurt Paucker's group in Philadelphia and had achieved results that were consistent with Gresser's findings.

duced in cells. The usefulness of interferon as a means of combatting some viral infections has already been convincingly demonstrated. In recent years the thought has developed that if interferon is effective against viruses, and if cancer may be a virus-caused disease, then perhaps interferon could be useful against malignant growths.

Experiments using interferon against various types of cancer are being carried out in Stockholm. Such work, if successful, could make a significant contribution to control of one of man's most dreaded diseases.[5]

Strander's decision to test interferon's effect on children and young adults who had osteogenic sarcoma stemmed from the fact that the therapy traditionally used at that time with this cancer gave predictably poor results: typically, 80 percent of patients treated with conventional surgery developed metastatic tumors that were invariably fatal. Strander believed that the high mortality rate of the cancer, its rapid course of disease, and the ineffectiveness of available therapy provided a situation in which it was both ethical and practical to test the efficacy of interferon. He designed a clinical trial protocol in which the interferon-treated patients would be compared with "historical controls," that is, the medical histories of patients who had been treated by other means before interferon's use. Historical controls were employed for two reasons: first, the number of patients was limited; and second, Strander felt that it was unethical to deny any possibly beneficial treatment to a patient for the sake of having concurrent controls. Unfortunately for Strander, this decision complicated the evaluation of results and had profound political ramifications.

The problem of historical controls was described by Dr. Arthur S. Levine, an oncologist who headed a panel of American physicians asked to evaluate Strander's data in 1975 by Dr. Vincent T. DeVita, Jr., then director of the Division of Cancer Chemotherapy, National Cancer Institute (NCI), who subsequently became director of the NCI. Levine explained:

I was suspicious that you couldn't compare results with osteosarcoma in the middle 1970s with what had happened in the middle 1960s and the middle 1930s. You had to prove that bona fide results were a function of treatment, as opposed to something else about the disease and its management or the selection of patients for a clinical trial. I asked Strander to send me all the data on his patients. I went over it in some detail with the people who were

5. *New York Times,* July 6, 1973.

on my committee.[6] It became apparent that [the trials] were comparing apples and oranges. I asked Hans [Strander] to pull together some concurrent control data—[from] patients being diagnosed and treated in Sweden now that were not coming to the Karolinska [Institute] for interferon. Several things became apparent.

First, bone tumors are very difficult to diagnose correctly. Some patients weren't true osteosarcoma; there was shifting diagnosis.

Second, this was not a homogeneously predictable disease. There were some grading variables and each variable provides very small prognostic weight. Only in looking at literally thousands of patients and doing a multivariate analysis would you realize their significance. Statistics in clinical research is still a relatively new thing, and twenty years ago, such analyses weren't performed.

Third, patients were selected differently for these clinical studies than historically.

Altogether, it becomes easy to understand that going from 20 percent to 40 percent disease-free survival is not very much and can be accounted for by problems of diagnostic interpretation [and] inadvertent skew due to prognostic variables, selection, and demography of referral.

Despite the uncertainties that caused Levine's fact-finding committee to conclude that optimism for interferon's use in osteogenic sarcoma was premature, the anecdotal reports of interferon's success by Strander propelled a number of scientists and laypersons to promote a national program for interferon research and development.

### Interferon Consciousness Raising: The 1975 Conference

Before the enactment of the National Cancer Act of 1971, a panel of consultants was assembled to advise the Senate Committee on Labor and Public Welfare on matters concerning the national cancer effort. A panel member who prepared a report on the status of cancer research was Dr. Mathilde Krim, a Swiss-born, Israeli-trained geneticist at New York's Memorial Sloan-Kettering Institute. In Dr. Krim's report, which was based on her study of the interferon literature, she concluded that interferon had potential as an antitumor agent and that it deserved further study. Krim's efforts in encouraging interest in interferon culminated in

6. The committee, chaired by Levine, then chief of Pediatric Oncology at the NCI, consisted of Richard Sarman, chief of the NCI Biostatistics Branch; Lewis Thomas, former head of the NCI pathology group; Dave Darlene, an eminent bone-tumor pathologist at the Mayo Clinic (Rochester, Minnesota), who had reported on hundreds of cases of osteosarcoma; and Jordan Wilbur, a well-known pediatric oncologist at Stanford University.

a conference organized by her in spring 1975. This meeting is now generally recognized as a turning point, after which national and international public attention was riveted on interferon.

Dr. Krim's firsthand experiences with the politics of American health research led her to attempt to raise the consciousness of both the scientific establishment and the American public about interferon.[7] This politically astute move had as its goal the engendering of support for interferon research. The lesson was soon clear, as described by Dr. Derek C. Burke, a British interferonologist:

> Interferon had become a political component of the American cancer scene. There were people like Mathilde [Krim] pushing hard for its development; there were other people in the NIH who were resisting. You have open lobbies in the United States, and these lobbies play an important role in how NCI money is spent. Mathilde's [1975] meeting in retrospect was a political exercise, designed to show people in senior positions in the NCI and in charities just how much potential there was. I don't blame Mathilde for this at all. Interferon still might be useful against cancer, and it was the way in which to get money into the field. But it's inevitably changed the character of the field because it became big money.

One of Dr. Krim's first major tasks was to develop funding for the 1975 conference. One group she approached was the NCI's Molecular Control Working Group, headed by Dr. Timothy O'Connor. The purpose of that group, which was established in February 1973 by the NCI director, Dr. Frank J. Rauscher, Jr., was to advise the director on new directions in molecular biology that might bear on the nation's anticancer effort. The group was to function outside bureaucratic channels; if the committee identified a new development with great potential, it had the power to circumvent the slow grant and contract system.

Drs. Strander and Cantell accompanied Dr. Krim on her visit to O'Connor. Recalling that visit, O'Connor said:

> They told me about the findings in the children [with osteogenic sarcoma] in Stockholm. My viewpoint was, here were fourteen kids who were apparently doing as well as had been found with the best methatrexate treatment at the time. I didn't think it important whether that was right or wrong. What I did think was important was that we as a national program would be delinquent if something came out of Europe that had been brought to our attention and

7. A more general discussion of the politics, including the relationships between the NIH, Congress, and special-interest groups, can be found in Stephen P. Strickland, *Politics, Science, and Dread Disease: A Short History of United States Medical Research Policy* (Harvard University Press, 1972).

we did nothing about it. I felt this should be evaluated on its own merits in the United States. I think this was basically the viewpoint of Mathilde [Krim].

When O'Connor advocated funding interferon work, however, he met opposition within the NCI. Thomas King, head of O'Connor's division, strenuously opposed circumventing the grant and peer review tradition. O'Connor was even told that some considered his plan to be illegal. O'Connor then took the issue directly to Rauscher, saying, "A cancer program exists: You, Dr. Rauscher, have set up a review committee; it has two Nobel laureates on it; you have fifteen eminent people. Let them advise you. You have authorization to go ahead. If there are fourteen kids walking around alive in Sweden, we shouldn't be thinking about [grants and review] channels."

O'Connor further recalled that the only real support he had was from C. Gordon Zubrod, an NCI scientist, who felt that "any good clinical thinking deserves clinical evaluation." Despite Rauscher's refusal to give major support to the interferon effort, the first international congress was held. O'Connor was never sure how the meeting was funded.[8]

O'Connor also recalled:

Mathilde [Krim] had more vision than I. She had representation of industry at those early meetings. I'm very impressed in retrospect. She had made this her cause and she was damn good at it. She had previously worked very closely with Benno Schmidt, putting the package together for the National Cancer Program. She did extremely well, much better than I could have done because, frankly, a private citizen can approach industry, whereas if a government guy did it in that environment at that time, we couldn't have been successful.

The solicitation of funds was not the only obstacle to Krim's conference. Some scientists were concerned that Krim was neither knowledgeable enough nor sufficiently critical to be interferon's champion. Others feared that she would gain too much control over the future course of interferon research. Still others were concerned that Krim's meeting would upstage an interferon conference organized by Dr. Thomas C. Merigan, a leading infectious disease specialist at Stanford University, that was scheduled to be held in fall 1975 at Stanford. Krim persisted, however, and eventually the three-day International Workshop on Interferon in the Treatment of Cancer was held at the Rockefeller Institute in New York City in April 1975.

8. The 1975 conference was supported in part by both the NIH and the private sector. Although industry may not have directly supported the conference, it was well represented.

Dr. Krim, in assessing the importance of the conference, said:

We had about two hundred people. For the first time clinicians, virologists, immunologists, oncologists, [and] NIH and NCI people were together. Then there was a meeting of the National Cancer Advisory Panel to review the conference report, and again very little came out of it, but not zero. The NCI agreed to buy $1 million worth of interferon. It was not very good interferon and they really didn't do anything more—they did not allocate more money or establish a cancer research emphasis grant program [to focus research effort on interferon]. But when the word interferon came up they didn't laugh anymore. It was consciousness raising. Nothing else had occurred [scientifically]. There was not one more shred of evidence in the literature [that interferon cured cancer].

By November 1975, Dr. Krim's report to the Board of Scientific Counselors of the NCI's Division of Cancer Treatment recommended that interferon be investigated as an antitumor agent. That same month, the National Cancer Advisory Board also recommended that the NCI purchase interferon for basic clinical studies.

One direct effect of the meeting—in addition to consciousness raising—was the first NCI-funded cancer trial with interferon. According to Krim,

The NCI wanted to put $1 million into something with interferon. I recommended we give Tom [Dr. Thomas C.] Merigan money for a prospective trial in lymphomas. The idea was to induce remission with a chemotherapeutic agent and try to maintain remission with interferon. This is the rational way to use interferon, but it is a long-term study. Merigan prepared the right protocol and was turned down. The NCI thought it was ridiculous to do a study for three years [because] "if interferon is any good we should know within one year." I pleaded that they reinstate the long-term trial and, fortunately, they agreed.

Although the April 1975 meeting was publicized as a workshop on interferon and cancer, the role of interferon as an antiviral agent was not overlooked. Under Dr. Martin S. Hirsch's direction at the Massachusetts General Hospital in Boston, experiments had been under way since 1973 to test whether interferon could be used prophylactically in mice to prevent virus activation following kidney transplantation. Dr. Hirsch and his colleagues had previously found that viral infections were exacerbated in the transplant setting. By 1975, he wanted to see if interferon would affect viral episodes in human renal transplant patients. Dr. Hirsch has commented:

It came to a head at Mathilde Krim's meeting in 1975. I literally pleaded for somebody to give me interferon for these parallel studies in humans. Cantell was interested and eventually provided us with the material. We started a trial in 1976. That [trial] finished in 1978 and was quite encouraging as far as being able to show that interferon prophylactically could reduce the incidence and probably the severity of cytomegalovirus and B-virus infections in these populations.

Although Hirsch recognized the importance of the 1975 meeting in generating support for interferon, he also acknowledged that only the positive aspects of interferon had so far been presented and that these were, in his words, "probably more laudatory, much more optimistic . . . than was justified at that time."

When asked why scientists such as himself did not protest the exaggerations about interferon's effectiveness, Hirsch noted:

It's easier for an individual to respond when whatever he's doing is being attacked than it is to respond when whatever it is he's doing is being praised without due basis. And I think that's really what happened. A lot of these people knew these claims about interferon were too exaggerated, but those overexaggerated claims succeeded in bringing in the money to the field to allow the advances that have subsequently been made in production, purification, and all that. True, it was at the expense of other areas that may have been just as profitable or more profitable to study. But it's awfully hard, I think, for someone to complain that he's getting too much money.

People who play a prominent role in mobilizing society for a new cause are almost by definition controversial. In catalyzing interest in interferon, Dr. Krim is no exception. Her detractors charge that she was insufficiently critical in her appraisal of the scientific validity of claims of interferon's usefulness in cancer treatment and that she pressed for a premature use of interferon in a clinical setting. However, much to her credit, the effort that she helped to organize resulted in a plethora of important scientific discoveries whose significance goes beyond the interferon field.

In addition to honest scientific differences with Krim over interferon's efficacy as a cancer drug, other factors have been felt to play a part in criticism of her. For example, O'Connor, in an interview with the author, mentioned the closeness of Krim and her husband to President Lyndon Johnson (Krim's husband was an important supporter of Johnson, as well as treasurer of the Democratic National Committee), plus the fact that Krim was a woman, as factors that may have worked against her.

*Support Builds for a Major Interferon Campaign*

Following the 1975 conference, the support of a number of key persons, as well as publicity surrounding several extrascientific events, fueled pressure for a major interferon campaign. First, the philanthropist Mary Lasker, whose vision and political skill have been crucial to the development of the NIH,[9] lent her support to the interferon effort. In addition, conservationist Laurence S. Rockefeller and Congressman Claude D. Pepper, Democrat of Florida, began to publicize interferon's potential. Dr. Alan S. Rabson, director of the NCI's Division of Cancer Biology and Diagnosis, who chaired a committee charged with procuring and distributing the $1 million worth of interferon purchased by the NCI, is reputed to have stopped to chat in an NCI corridor with Mary Lasker and Laurence Rockefeller. In response to Rabson's commenting on an associate of Rockefeller's who, having cancer and failing to respond to various treatments, had received interferon, Rockefeller is reported to have noted that the person had died and that it was "a case of too little interferon given too late"!

A development that unwittingly aided the cause was the publicity given the diagnosis of osteogenic sarcoma in Senator Edward Kennedy's son. Interferon was immediately installed in the nation's headlines because Kennedy's tumor was reported to be the kind on which Strander had experimented. This publicity focused attention on the difficulty and cost of manufacturing interferon in the quantities necessary for clinical application.

Another person who played an important role in promoting the use of interferon in cancer patients was Dr. Jordan Gutterman, of the M. D. Anderson Hospital and Tumor Institute in Houston. After learning of interferon as a potential cancer therapeutic at Krim's 1975 conference, Gutterman became an advocate of the clinical use of interferon. Encouraged in his efforts by Mary Lasker and her associate Deeda McCormick Blair, Gutterman soon realized that only dramatic measures would enable his clinical program to obtain sufficient funds to purchase interferon. Although some interferon produced in Cantell's laboratory in Helsinki had been purchased with NCI's $1 million, the interferon was already being spread too thinly among six clinical centers. According to Gutterman,

> There weren't any real solid data to justify what was required—a large capital investment. Now, how do you get someone, the government, to put $5 or $10

9. Lasker's role in the development of the National Cancer Institute and the National Heart, Lung, and Blood Institute is described in Richard A. Rettig, *Cancer Crusade: The Story of the National Cancer Act of 1971* (Princeton University Press, 1977); Natalie Davis Spingarn, *Heartbeat: The Politics of Health Research* (Washington, D.C.: Robert B. Luce, 1976); and Strickland, *Politics, Science, and Dread Disease.*

million into interferon clinical research if no data existed? We were caught in a total Catch-22 situation. How do you get out of it? You get out of it, I guess, the way we did. Mary Lasker said, "We've got to do something, I'm tired of waiting." . . . So she called me in the summer of 1977 and said, "The [Albert and Mary Lasker] Foundation will have to start the support."

The Albert and Mary Lasker Foundation provided $1 million for the purchase of additional interferon for Gutterman's clinical program. One factor in Lasker's decision to provide the funds is said to have been the illness of one of her associates, who suffered from cancer and was not responding to chemotherapy. As Lasker began to realize the limitations of conventional tumor therapy, she became eager to encourage new approaches to cancer treatment.

## The ACS Commitment

By this time, Frank J. Rauscher, Jr., had resigned as director of the NCI and had become senior vice president for research at the American Cancer Society's (ACS) national headquarters in New York City. Under Rauscher's aegis the ACS turned into a leading proponent of the experimental use of interferon in cancer. Speaking about the circumstances that surrounded the ACS's decision in 1978 to finance clinical trials of interferon, Rauscher said:

Jordan [Gutterman] was very important at that time, because he had enough guts to write up a proposal for $2 million. He and I talked on the phone and I encouraged him to do this. I said, "Why don't you send it in and let me at least take a look at your summary data." I was sitting here one Friday afternoon with all of this sort of brewing, and I thought, "We've got to do something about this. There are no controlled trials anywhere in the world. If there is enough material to be made available by Finland, let's buy some [interferon] and convene a group that will advise the society [ACS]." That afternoon I went upstairs and told my boss, Lane Adams, "We'd better bite this bullet," which we did, and within about five weeks I presented this to a subcommittee of our board, and they agreed [to] an initial investment of $2 million, at $50 a million [interferon] units. I was in a very good spot to sell it. I was probably known as the most negative interferon person in the country because [previously] I didn't recommend, and I could have, that the NCI commit $5 million.

Why did Rauscher turn bullish on interferon when earlier as NCI director he refused to make a major commitment? When asked the reason, Rauscher mentioned that he had been swayed by several new developments, such as information from cancer specialists in the United States that interferon may indeed have shown an effect in some forms of cancer "in maybe eight to ten patients."

The 1978 ACS decision to spend $2 million to purchase interferon triggered an avalanche of interferon-related publicity. The ACS's interferon budget was heralded as the largest amount of money ever committed by the society for a single project. This fact was obviously not lost on the media. If an important national society devoted to the conquest of cancer had considered interferon worthy, something of great significance was likely to be happening. Was it possible that the long-elusive cancer cure was finally at hand? This unrealistic hope was, perhaps inadvertently, corroborated by some well-meaning but not very critical statements in the media. The impression conveyed almost universally was that thousands of lives could be saved if only enough interferon were available.[10]

Concerning the exaggerated press coverage that surrounded the first large-scale clinical cancer trials in 1980–82, Dr. Gutterman recalled:

We paid heavily in terms of all this [publicity]—the demands on patients, the disappointments when we didn't have a cure. . . . If you read the articles through, no one ever claimed anything that wasn't there. But cancer being the emotional problem that it is, it was way overplayed. But it has been good from the standpoints of accelerating a lot of interest and [generating] money. There is a lot of private money in this research. . . . I think Congress moved on it in part because of the publicity. In total, it's kind of evened-out, settled down. Now the field is getting on a very solid scientific ground, certainly in basic research and gradually in clinical research. But it was pretty rough there for a while.

Rauscher recalled that by December 1981 the ACS had spent $6 million on its interferon program. He announced that the ACS had essentially completed its interferon program and had achieved its three original objectives, which were, first, to determine if interferon could be shown to have any anticancer activity at all when put to an objective test by American cancer specialists; second, to find out how interferon is

10. Some typical newspaper headlines in the late 1970s included: "Interferon Viewed as Next Treatment Breakthrough"; "Interferon: The IF Drug for Cancer"; "Interferon: The Cancer Drug We've Ignored"; "Wonder Cancer Drug: Even Shah Couldn't Buy It."

best administered to patients—that is, how much should be given and when it should be given, how it works, whether it might work better in combination with other drugs, and so forth; and third, to see whether the U.S. government and American industry could be induced to back interferon research. Definitive answers to the first two objectives are still forthcoming. The third goal was achieved brilliantly, however. As is described in chapters 3 and 4, the federal government and private industry have escalated their interest in interferon since the inception of the ACS program in 1978.

In addition, other resources were mobilized to continue testing interferon in man. A private foundation that has provided support for clinical testing of interferon is the Interferon Foundation. Incorporated in 1980 as a not-for-profit foundation, its sole aim is to purchase interferon for use in clinical trials. The motivating force behind the foundation is its president, Leon Davis, an independent Houston oilman who was first alerted to interferon in early 1979 by his wife after she read a *Time* magazine article on interferon's potential anticancer properties.[11] After inquiring of physician friends, Davis was put in contact with Jordan Gutterman, on whose recommendation and advice the Interferon Foundation was established. As of March 1983, $10 million had been raised, mainly from the oil industry, for the purchase of interferon. Davis believes that this is the largest sum ever raised privately for a single drug. He also believes that the foundation will need to raise an additional $10 million before its goal—eliminating the cost of interferon as an obstacle in its clinical evaluation—is reached. Asked about the effects of these funds, Davis said that he found the interferon field five years ahead of where it would have been without his foundation's work. The three classes of interferons—alpha, beta, and gamma—can be made either by recombinant-DNA techniques or by more tedious methods whereby interferon is extracted at great expense from cell cultures. The Interferon Foundation purchases only Cantell-type interferon-alpha and interferon-gamma (both extracted from human cell cultures), because by spring 1983 the manufacturers of recombinant interferon-alpha were providing their products gratis for clinical trial use. The foundation believes that if, as a result of their purchase, the Cantell-type interferon-alpha and interferon-gamma are used more extensively in clinical trials and are found to be effective, then industry in turn will be stimulated to produce more of these products.

11. *Time* (November 6, 1978), p. 68.

## Interferon and the Genetic Revolution: 1979–83

In late 1979 the nature of interferon research was altered radically. Dr. Tadatsugu Taniguchi, working at the not-for-profit Japanese Cancer Research Institute, outside Tokyo, reported the successful cloning of a human interferon gene.[12] Within eighteen months of this event, over twenty distinct human interferon genes were isolated. And though much of the work was generated in university facilities, the race to clone interferon represented major efforts of new genetic engineering companies or collaborations between universities and either drug houses or genetic engineering firms. This intimate linking of industry and academe blurred the distinction between the two sectors. The commercial interest in interferon attracted public attention, and as a result, the discussion about how to define the relationship between industry and academe has centered on interferon.

It is now apparent that interferon was chosen as the most visible demonstration project of the newly developing biotechnology industry. How did this occur? As the interferon effort increased with the ACS's support in 1978, the embryonic genetic engineering industry was on the verge of becoming the subject of much attention by the popular press. Genetic engineering—including recombinant-DNA technology—uses discoveries made in the early 1970s that allow scientists to identify and isolate portions of the genetic material (DNA) that contain the information to direct the production of specific proteins. Once isolated, the DNA is transferred into bacteria or other microorganisms where the protein can be produced in almost unlimited quantities and then extracted in pure form. The allure of this technology is that a human or animal protein that is scarce, like interferon, can be made in quantity quite inexpensively.

By 1978 several private biotechnology companies had been formed with the active participation of leading university-based scientists. The new companies, including Genentech and Cetus Corporation in California and the Geneva, Switzerland–based Biogen, were poised to prove

12. T. Taniguchi and others, "Construction and Identification of a Bacterial Plasmid Containing the Human Fibroblast Interferon Gene Sequence," *Proceedings of the Japanese Academy of Science*, series B: *Physical and Biological Sciences*, vol. 55, no. 9 (1979), pp. 464–69.

the worth of their newly developed technologies. The cloning of interferon was a project ideally suited for this purpose.

In choosing a protein to be a demonstration project, several criteria
had to be met. First, a potential commercial market was required for the
product. Second, the product made by genetic engineering techniques
would have to be less expensive than material produced by the conventional technology used in 1978. Third, and most important, methods
were required that would allow the isolation of the chosen protein's
DNA to be monitored accurately.[13]

Biological assays for interferon had been in use since interferon's
discovery. The assays were easy and rapid enough to correctly detect
isolated interferon DNA. When the hopes for interferon as both an
antiviral agent and an antitumor drug suggested a potentially enormous
market, interferon became an attractive demonstration project. Only a
short list of other biologicals—human growth hormone, several proteins
identified for use as human vaccines, and human insulin—met all the
criteria to become demonstration projects for the new technology. Eli
Lilly and Company, a major producer of porcine insulin, selected insulin
as its first genetic engineering project.[14] Several other large, established
pharmaceutical companies, foremost among them Hoffmann-La Roche,
Schering-Plough Corporation, and G. D. Searle and Company, joined
the young biotechnology firms in selecting interferon as the demonstration project.

13. The genetic engineering of biologicals using bacteria can be divided conceptually
into four steps. First, the correct DNA must be isolated. Second, the DNA must be put
into the bacteria, which can then produce the desired protein. Third, the bacteria must
be grown in large quantity. Fourth, the protein must be purified. The third and fourth
steps employ procedures that have been used by the pharmaceutical industry for over
fifty years. The first and second steps were products of the 1970s' revolution. By far
the most difficult step is the first—identifying the correct DNA. The DNA for a single
interferon gene represents less than 0.0000001 percent of total cellular DNA. Therefore,
it was imperative to have a convenient assay to assure the successful isolation of the
desired gene.

14. See "Insulin Wars: New Advances May Throw Market into Turbulence,"
*Science,* vol. 210 (December 12, 1980), pp. 1225–28. Eli Lilly's control over a $100-
million-per-year insulin market was reported to be threatened by two Danish firms
(Novo and Nordisk) that had prepared highly purified porcine insulin and had a vehicle
for its delivery. Lilly, understandably, was interested in maintaining its market and,
with Genentech, had established a collaboration to buy genetic engineering expertise
and produce human insulin. The product, Humulin, was the first and only genetically
engineered biological on the market as of January 1983. If patent protection is upheld,
Humulin will guarantee Lilly's market position.

The large drug houses invested in interferon in one of two ways. One approach, exemplified by the G. D. Searle effort, emphasized in-house research. The other approach was to buy genetic engineering expertise—for example, Hoffmann-La Roche's collaboration with Genentech on interferon-alpha. Similarly, Schering-Plough purchased equity in Biogen and signed a right-of-first-refusal agreement to produce some of Biogen's projected products, principal among them interferon.

How much did the publicity generated by the "interferon lobby"—Krim, Lasker, Gutterman, and the ACS—influence the decision of these companies to enter the race to clone interferon? Gutterman agrees with Rauscher that the media attention given interferon after the announcement of the ACS support whetted industry's appetite for interferon:

> I think one positive thing it did [ACS support and concomitant media attention] was [that] it got the image of interferon to industry in a big way. I'm not sure we'd have all the progress if it hadn't been for what's coming out of the recombinant-DNA area. What gene do you clone? Why interferon rather than some other genes? I remember going to Hoffmann-La Roche before the publicity in 1978 with Mary Lasker. They had an interferon program. I don't know what resources were going into it but I can guarantee [the resources] doubled or tripled after they saw what was happening. Eventually, that culminated in some of the arrangements with Genentech.

Media hype also affected the decision of small genetic boutiques to focus on interferon. Dr. Zsolt Harsanyi, of E. F. Hutton, said that the ability of these new companies to secure venture capital was intimately associated with their decision to clone interferon (see chapter 4).

The power of the media was quickly capitalized upon by the for-profit genetic engineers. Although the first successful cloning of a human interferon gene was accomplished at the Japanese Cancer Research Institute, this feat was swiftly overshadowed in the press by the enormous publicity given the first successful production of small quantities of active human interferon in bacteria by a team headed by Biogen's Charles Weissmann, working from his laboratory at the University of Zurich.[15] Biogen's announcement of the production of active interferon in bacteria exemplifies the change in how progress in biomedical research is communicated. On January 16, 1980, Biogen and Schering-Plough staged a joint press conference at the Park Plaza Hotel in Boston.

15. Weissmann's status as a founding member of Biogen and his somewhat unorthodox use of a university laboratory for a commercially oriented project have focused attention on conflicts of interest that arise when professors become entrepreneurs (see chapter 4).

Invitations sent to the media for this event promised that news of great importance would be disclosed. Walter Gilbert, a Nobel prizewinner who in 1980 was a Harvard professor and chairman of Biogen's scientific board, told the media about Weissmann's successful cloning of one type of human interferon. The press conference set off an international wave of interferon publicity, in which the achievement was described in terms such as the solution to manufacturing a "priceless miracle drug." The January 16 press conference coincided with a temporary eight-point rise in Schering-Plough's stock and had been preceded a few months earlier by Biogen's reassessment of its value from $50 million to $100 million.[16] Within a short time, interferon was on the cover of *Time* magazine.[17]

The successful cloning of interferon fundamentally changed the interferon field in two ways. First, much of the research effort, including basic research, shifted to the private sector (see chapter 4). And second, the field experienced an information explosion. In less than two years, more information about the fundamental properties of interferon was generated than in the preceding twenty-odd years since interferon's discovery.

## Interferon after 1983

The greatest impetus to the development of interferon resulted from the expectation that it might cure cancer. As emphasized earlier, the first problem to solve was that of the interferon supply. In 1976 the world supply of interferon allowed only a few patients to receive therapy. As of 1983 over thirty corporations in the United States alone were engaged in producing interferon. Not only is interferon produced for intravenous injection, topical application, and inoculations into the brain, but an interferon-containing toothpaste is even being developed in Japan. Clinical trials of interferon's efficacy in viral diseases, in various tumors, in multiple sclerosis, and in other diseases characterized by disorders of the immune system are in progress.

Will interferon be useful therapeutically? As of 1983 thousands of cancer patients have received interferon produced either by conventional

16. "Cloning Gold Rush Turns Basic Biology into Big Business," *Science*, vol. 208 (May 16, 1980), pp. 688–92.
17. "The Big IF in Cancer," *Time* (March 31, 1980), pp. 60–66.

methods (such as the Cantell procedure, using white blood cells) or by recombinant-DNA technology. In trials using Cantell-style interferon, the tumors of some patients with myeloma, lymphoma, breast cancer, and malignant melanoma have shown some shrinkage. But the results have been inconsistent: most patients have not responded at all, and the tumors of others have shown only transient or minor reductions in size.

Since Cantell-style interferon contains a mixture of interferons and many "impurities," the more pure and homogeneous preparations produced by recombinant-DNA technology were expected to give better and more consistent results. However, reports on the first extensive group of patients to receive recombinant interferon, announced at the April 1982 meeting of the American Society of Clinical Oncology, were disappointing. Only a small percentage of cancer patients showed a partial decrease in tumor size. Still, it must be stressed that these phase-one trials were of limited duration,[18] and it was unclear how long therapy had to be continued before results could be declared negative. Dr. Stephen Sherwin, who was the principal investigator in trials with recombinant interferon that were sponsored by the NCI, and who has since joined Genentech, said, "Because a large variety of cancers were treated at very different doses, no definite statements can yet be made with regard to how effective this interferon might be for a specific type of cancer."

More recent studies with recombinant interferon yielded another unpleasant surprise. Although one of the principal virtues of interferon was thought to be its lack of toxicity, all interferon preparations tested in patients so far have been found to produce side effects. Most patients treated with interferon develop fever, chills, fatigue, loss of appetite, a decrease in white-blood-cell counts, and—with prolonged administration—some hair loss. These side effects are generally reversible and less

18. In the process of gathering information on a new drug to be approved for sale by the FDA, a series of clinical trials are conducted. Human testing is divided into three phases (not to be confused with the three phases of scientific research and development described in chapter 1). In phase one, testing in a limited number of patients (20–80) is directed toward learning how the chemical acts in the body and if further testing should be done (that is, pharmacokinetics [dose and schedule] and indication of efficacy). In phase two, attempts are made to show usefulness in a specific disease in generally no more than 200 persons. In phase three, extensive tests are done under conditions that would be recommended if the drug were approved. For more description, see Wayne L. Pines, "A Primer on New Drug Development," HEW Publication (FDA) 81-3021 (July 1981).

severe than those arising from most other forms of cancer chemotherapy, but it is evident that interferon is not as harmless as some of its advocates had thought. As interferon research shifts to exploring the role of interferon as a regulator of the immune response, these side effects emerge as possible aberrations of immune regulation.

As early as the middle 1970s, hints of interferon's possible negative side effects had emerged that were not highly publicized. Dr. Alphonse Billiau, a Belgian interferonologist in Leuven, recalled an incident at an international interferon meeting in Israel in 1977.[19] Dr. Billiau's colleague and mentor, Dr. Pieter De Somer, arrived at the meeting concerned because severe side effects had been observed following administration of interferon to a Belgian patient. The response to this news by some was that such negative results should not be made generally public because they would dampen popular enthusiasm for interferon and stall the interferon crusade just as it was gaining momentum.[20] In addition, several articles written by Dr. Billiau in an attempt to alert the general medical community to the side effects were rejected for publication, including an editorial cynically entitled, "Interferon's War on Cancer: A Bag of Hot Air?"

Another problem with side effects surfaced in France in November 1982, when four patients being treated with interferon that was made at the Pasteur Institute in Paris died of heart attacks. As a result, the French government suspended clinical trials of Cantell-style interferon produced by the institute. Professor Robert Flamant, president of a committee supervising the trials, suggested that either a problem in the manufacture of the interferon, or a problem with the drug itself, or an unlucky series of coincidences might explain the deaths. According to the *Washington Post,* "Asked if there had been similar problems in tests in other countries, Professor Flamant said: 'Tolerance to interferon is not as good as was thought a few years ago, but no one has informed us of accidents of the type we have experienced.' "[21]

Shortly afterward an article in *Science* magazine noted: "Meanwhile,

19. The Fifth Aharon Katzir–Katchalsky Conference: Symposium on Interferons and The Control of Cell-Virus Interactions, Rehovot, Israel, May 2–6, 1977.
20. This anecdote has parallels in many other scientific debates. When should scientific information be made public, especially if the information is controversial and has not been extensively confirmed? What are the ethics of disclosing or withholding information about the possible deleterious effects of a substance? For further discussion, see chapter 5.
21. Quoted in the *Washington Post,* November 5, 1982.

the deaths of four patients have helped stir a growing debate over whether it is ethical to permit experimentation on human subjects on such a large scale before more detailed information is known about the therapeutic action of interferon and its toxic side effects."[22] This article and other publicity surrounding the deaths prompted the NCI's director of the biological response modifiers program (BRMP),[23] Dr. Robert K. Oldham, to respond with a detailed outline of the NCI's experience with interferon toxicity. "It is important," said Oldham, "for investigators to recognize that interferons can have toxic effects and that certain exclusions for preexisting problems are appropriate."[24]

The realization that interferon is not harmless coincided with additional findings that interferon might be responsible for some disease symptoms in virus infections and in disorders of the immune system. For example, patients who suffer from systemic lupus erythematosus, a disease characterized by a malfunctioning immune system, have been shown to produce increased levels of interferon. It is possible that increased interferon production in lupus patients may aggravate the disease by causing further disturbances of immune functions. For example, some lupus patients spontaneously make antibodies to interferon. Production of antibodies to normal body proteins is considered to be one of the mechanisms of pathology in this disease.

Similarly, hyperproduction of interferon has been found in patients with acquired immunodeficiency syndrome (AIDS), a mysterious group of diseases that, by mid-1983, had been much publicized, owing to its epidemic proportions. Some AIDS patients develop a cancer known as Kaposi's sarcoma, and it has been suggested that interferon treatment might be effective on these patients. The use of experimental interferon therapy in AIDS patients has become the focus of controversy as attention is paid increasingly to the possible disease-inducing role of interferon. In some patients interferon may be not only ineffective but harmful, because it may weaken a patient's ability to resist cancer if it is administered indiscriminately.

22. "Deaths Halt Interferon Trials in France," *Science,* vol. 218 (November 19, 1982), p. 772.

23. As is described in chapter 3, since 1978 work on interferon supported by the NCI has been coordinated by the biological response modifers program. The term *biological response modifier* was coined to indicate that the activity of a substance would be to modify or regulate a biological response. Interferon is a prototype and is now being studied as a "regulator" of the immune response.

24. Robert K. Oldham, as quoted in "Death Halts Interferon Trials in France."

Will interferon ever cure cancer? The consensus among scientists is that interferon, by itself, is not likely to replace or even rival other, already available forms of treatment. Yet hope persists that some forms of interferon might be more powerful than those already tested, or that some varieties of cancer that respond more readily to interferon may be identified.[25] Furthermore, given the finding that many forms of interferon exist, it is possible that specific interferons could be tailored to specific tumors. Interferon may also prove useful in treating some tumors if applied in combination with other anticancer drugs. More research and clinical trials are needed to test these possibilities. The successes are likely to be considerably more modest than the miraculous cures prophesied in 1980, but almost no one is willing to dismiss the potential worth of interferon.

Although cancer seems to have so far eluded interferon's reach, other disorders appear to respond. One of these is the common wart, a benign tumor caused by viral infection. The producers of recombinant interferon may find that their products, originally intended for the cure of cancer, will be used instead against virus infections—the infections that the drug was first observed to control, long before cancer took precedence as the object of interferon therapy. Interferon has been effective in some conventional virus diseases such as severe infections by varicella zoster and cytomegalovirus.

Mathilde Krim has been criticized because interferon has not proved to be the panacea she hoped it would be. Yet the interferon crusade, which was largely inspired by the conference she organized, has in a very short time yielded important scientific discoveries of significance beyond the interferon field itself. In 1975 clinicians like Dr. Martin S. Hirsch literally had to beg for enough impure interferon for their studies. In 1983 it was common to hear presentations at scientific meetings accompanied by photographs of highly purified crystals of interferon weighing several milligrams.

25. According to a memorandum from Frank J. Rauscher, Jr., to the staff of the American Cancer Society, interferon-alpha is being used with some success to treat kidney cancer. The update stated: " 'Alpha-interferon appears highly promising in treating kidney cancer, and it may well prove to be the most effective single agent against this form of cancer,' says Dr. Jules Harris of the Illinois Cancer Council. . . . Kidney cancer is also being studied by researchers at Yale University, M. D. Anderson Hospital in Houston, and UCLA. The interferon treatment looks better than chemotherapy, hormonal, or immunotherapy for kidney cancer, says Dr. de Kernion, a surgeon/ urologist who is also director of clinical programs at the Johnson UCLA Cancer Center."

Some of the new information about interferon was surprising. It was known, for example, that interferon could be divided into three general classes, and so it was expected that genetic engineers would isolate three different interferon genes. Instead, about twenty different interferon genes had been isolated from human cells by the fall of 1981. Since then, these genes have been extensively characterized by molecular genetic techniques. The interferons are now divided into three groups—interferon-alpha, interferon-beta, and interferon-gamma. While all interferons are carbohydrate-containing proteins, and all share the ability to protect cells in the laboratory from virus infection, they nevertheless exhibit functional and structural differences.

The finding that there are many interferons complicates enormously their study and clinical application. The early clinical trials were performed using interferon preparations whose composition in terms of the various interferon species was unknown. But now certain questions must be answered, such as which interferons have similar or different functions, and which interferon(s) should be tested clinically, and in what diseases. Stephen K. Carter, vice president in charge of anticancer research at Bristol-Myers Company, commented:

> Now clinical investigators are faced with an embarrassment of riches as multiple interferons are available in large quantity. It appears that the clinical study of interferons could become an industry unto itself. This places a great responsibility on both the National Cancer Institute and the pharmaceutical industry in the United States to develop some guidelines and end points for phase one, two, and three clinical trials. Currently, a feverish competition exists as many new biotechnology firms are producing interferons for clinical study either alone or in collaboration with pharmaceutical companies. Some of the major cancer research centers in the United States are . . . studying as many as five different interferon preparations. . . . It is already obvious that interferon by itself is not a major breakthrough in cancer therapy. If it is to have a role at all, it will most likely be within the framework of a combined-modality integration. This role cannot be established by clinical trials grounded in "home-run" mentality. Unless some order is achieved within the current chaotic situation, there is a high risk that the true role of interferon may not be found.[26]

Once considered pseudoscience, the biochemistry and genetics of the interferon system are now among the most thoroughly understood

26. "The Clinical Trial Evaluation Strategy for Interferons and Other Biological Response Modifers—Not a Simple Task," *Journal of Biological Response Modifiers,* vol. 1, no. 2 (1982), p. 105.

biological systems. Findings from interferon studies are fundamentally altering concepts relating to the core issues of contemporary biology— for example, our understanding of how gene expression in mammalian cells is controlled. Interferons are involved not only in the regulation of immunity but also, possibly, in embryonic development, growth regulation, and nerve function. Five or ten years from now, the information gained from interferon research is likely to have a dramatic effect on the practice of medicine.

## Chapter Three

# Funding Interferon

The reasoning behind the decisions by the federal government and private industry to invest in interferon research and development is described and analyzed in this chapter. The technological advances as well as the limitations of interferon research are discussed, along with consideration of extrascientific events. The discussion emphasizes how fascination with a potential cancer cure drove researchers, investors, and the business community to concentrate on interferon.

Federal funding of interferon by the National Institutes of Health is outlined for the period 1972–82, as are the mechanisms used to implement the federal interferon effort. Three distinct periods of federal expenditures are identified. The first, from 1972 to 1975, begins with the decision to develop interferon as a prototype antiviral agent and ends with the recognition that research had been stalled by technological limitations. The second period, from 1975 to 1978, opens with Mathilde Krim's 1975 landmark conference and the ensuing campaign to revive interferon's image as a research area worthy of major attention. This period closes with the decision by industry to use interferon as its main demonstration project to test the commercial viability of genetic engineering in the production of pharmaceuticals. The third period, from 1979 to 1982, sees an explosion of information about interferon at the molecular and clinical levels. The period ends with many questions still unresolved regarding the use and effectiveness of interferon as a drug.

The costs of developing interferon and the federal contribution to industrial efforts are considered, with discussion focusing throughout on how industrial and governmental decisions are often parallel or interactive. Several cost-effective instruments used by the government to stimulate interferon's development are described: (1) the establishment of standard research reagents, (2) the mediation of rapid information exchange through the *Interferon Scientific Memoranda (ISM)*, and (3) the convening of consensus conferences. These mechanisms had the effect of fostering technology transfer from public laboratories to the private sector. And to further encourage industry participation, the government acted to provide an early market by purchasing industrially made interferon for research and early clinical trials.

## Federal Involvement in Interferon

Interferon research has been conducted in academic, commercial, and federal laboratories with the support of federal funds. Although many federal agencies have supported interferon research, most federal funds have come from the NIH. For the purposes of this discussion, federal support is defined as NIH support.

Although individual interferon research projects were supported by the NIH during the 1960s, before 1969 interferon did not receive special emphasis. Interferon research was done both through the intramural program at NIH facilities ("in-house research"—for example, in Bethesda, Maryland, and at the Frederick Cancer Research Center) and through the extramural program where work was performed on university campuses, in independent not-for-profit research laboratories, and in commercial laboratories. At that time, all interferon extramural research was assigned to the National Institute of Allergy and Infectious Diseases. In the late 1960s, as a result of improvements in interferon purification and anecdotal experiments in man, interest in interferon as a broad-spectrum antiviral agent was heightened and a formal interferon program at the NIAID was established in 1969. This program, known as the antiviral substances program, in the NIAID's Development and Applications Branch (DAB), was part of the extramural research program.[1] A formal interferon program within the National Cancer Institute was not established until ten years later.[2]

Although many viral infections occur without long-term health consequences (for example, common colds, influenza), the communicability of many infections and the possibility of more serious complications if infections go untreated make viral diseases a leading public health

1. The DAB evolved from the Vaccine Development Branch at NIH, which, with the establishment of the antiviral substances program, became the Infectious Disease Branch. In 1977, following reorganization of the NIAID, the program became part of the DAB. For simplicity, the interferon program commencing in 1969 will be called DAB throughout the discussion.
2. The biological response modifiers program (BRMP), of which interferon was the cornerstone, was established in 1978.

concern. There are still no preventive measures for many viral diseases. Even the new, long-awaited hepatitis vaccine is effective for only a small percentage of viral-caused hepatitis. In addition, many other diseases (such as multiple sclerosis, juvenile diabetes, and some leukemias) are suspected of having viral etiologies. The development of antiviral drugs thus remains a goal with substantial economic and public health benefits.

When the NIAID established its interferon program, the association of a virus with its host cell was just beginning to be understood at the molecular level. Viruses, defined as obligate intracellular parasites, usurp their host cells' biochemical apparatus (in other words, the cells' energy-generating machinery, apparatus for producing proteins, nutrient supply, and so forth) to generate progeny virus. Successful viral replication frequently results in the destruction of the host cell.

The recognition that viruses use the host cells' biochemical machinery created a conceptual problem for the development of antiviral drugs. Many virologists reasoned that a drug that would inhibit viral replication would also inhibit normal cell processes. They argued that the most that could be expected from any antiviral drug would be conditions of "differential toxicity"—the antiviral drug would be very toxic for infected cells but would have little toxicity for uninfected cells. Interferon, on the other hand, was thought to be a natural substance whose only function was to fight viral infections without being toxic to uninfected cells. It therefore seemed to be the ideal antiviral agent.

Dorland J. Davis, with the NIAID's extramural program, was interested in establishing whether interferon could be used clinically. He wanted, moreover, to make interferon visible and a focus of NIAID research. In 1969, therefore, he recruited George J. Galasso, a professor of microbiology at the University of Virginia, to head the NIAID antiviral substances program, which was to be directed primarily to interferon. Galasso recalled:

> The initial intent of the DAB was to work on interferon: how you can make it, the development of standards, to find what the holes were in interferon research and to plug them using the contract mechanism. From 1969 on, we supported a lot of interferon research in terms of NIAID's budget. We started with approximately a million dollars and we never went much beyond three million.[3]

3. During 1972–82, the time period analyzed for this report, the lowest level of NIAID's interferon funding occurred in 1975, when $1.5 million was expended for interferon research, representing 2.1 percent of the NIAID's research budget. The highest expenditure from the NIAID occurred in 1979, when $2.9 million was spent, representing 3.3 percent of the NIAID budget. *NIH Data Book, 1982.*

Galasso, while interested in interferon, saw it only as the cornerstone of a national effort to support the development of antiviral agents. In a memorandum to NIAID's management (June 25, 1969), which formally suggested the DAB's establishment, Galasso noted:

> After twelve years [since interferon's discovery] . . . . we do not really know what [interferon] is or how it works. . . . [Yet] there is at present sufficient knowledge . . . to warrant an active program to solve the interferon problem and determine its future. Because of its role in infectious diseases . . . [a program] should be undertaken by the NIAID Collaborative Program. . . . If the interferon research proves fruitless the program can divert its resources to other antiviral substances. The emphasis of this program should be on the complete interferon problem. It should not simply be an extension of intramural research, field trials, screening, etc. . . . it should act as liaison for all the interferon work done by the intramural scientists and supported by the extramural branch, as well as work done by the NCI. . . . The program . . . should support basic research that is not being supported by the extramural program or which needs further work.

The NIH used a battery of mechanisms to support interferon work in its intramural and extramural research programs (see table 3-1). For the purposes of this analysis, funding instruments used in the extramural program are grouped into two categories: awards initiated by the NIH and responded to by investigators (in other words, directed or targeted research funds, which for simplicity will be called contracts) and those initiated by the investigator (in other words, nontargeted funds, here referred to as grants). Work supported by nontargeted funds is often mistakenly equated with basic research, as opposed to work supported by targeted instruments, which is viewed as applied research. In fact, the distinction has less to do with the scientific content of the work supported than with the way in which the funding is initiated and with how closely the NIH monitors the course of research (contract research is monitored more strenuously). It is true, however, that some efforts (such as procurement of research reagents, human experimentation, and so forth) may be most often supported by contract funds. In the next section the federal funding of interferon is compared with that of biomedical research in general, providing perspective on the priority attached to interferon in the overall science effort.

*Patterns of Research Funding*

Figures 3-1 and 3-2 compare interferon funding with general biomedical science research funding in current and constant 1972 dollars

Table 3-1. *Federal Funding Instruments Used*
*for Interferon Research, 1972–82*

| Instrument | Number | Definition |
|---|---|---|
| *Investigator-initiated grants* | | |
| P01 | 199 | Research program projects |
| P30 | 33 | Center core grants |
| P02 | 15 | Categorical clinical research center (phased out by 1975) |
| P15 | 3 | Occupational clinical research center (phased out by 1975) |
| P50 | 14 | Specialized center |
| P60 | 1 | Comprehensive center |
| R01 | 765 | Research project (grants) |
| R10 | 5 | Cooperative clinical research (grants) |
| R13 | 3 | Conferences (traditional) |
| R21 | 4 | Exploratory-developmental grants |
| R22 | 15 | United States–Japan cooperative medical science program |
| R23 | 23 | New investigator research awards |
| R26 | 9 | National organ site projects (National Cancer Institute) |
| S06 | 5 | Minority biomedical support (Division of Research Resources) |
| *Government-initiated contracts* | | |
| M01 | 67 | General clinical research centers |
| N01 | 178 | Research and project contracts |
| U10 | 3 | Cooperative clinical research (cooperative agreements) |
| *Work done in government laboratories* | | |
| Z01 | 193 | Intramural projects |

Sources: Activity codes, organizational codes, and definitions used in extramural programs, National Institutes of Health Manual Issuance 4101, October 1981. Data derived from the NIH CRISP data base, 1972–82.

between 1972 and 1982. This period has been chosen not only because the targeted interferon program within NIAID allowed interferon-specific spending to be identified in the NIAID budget for these years, but also because 1971 was the first year included in the computerized IMPAC and CRISP data bases.[4] More important, significant variations in interferon funding occurred during 1972–82 that can be attributed to specific scientific and extrascientific developments.

Each entry in the CRISP data base contains an abstract describing the purpose and plan of research. The abstract is prepared by the

4. The Statistics and Analysis Branch within the Division of Research Grants operates IMPAC and CRISP, two computer-based information systems at NIH. IMPAC (Information for Management Planning Analysis and Coordination) is the primary reporting source for administrative aspects of extramural programs. CRISP (Computer Retrieval of Information on Scientific Projects) supplies data on research grants and contracts conducted extramurally. From 1975 on, CRISP has also compiled data on NIH intramural projects.

Figure 3-1.  *Extramural Expenditures by the National Institutes of Health for Interferon Research and Production, Fiscal Years 1972–82*[a]

Millions

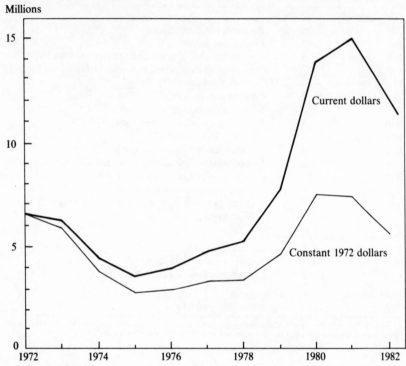

Source: Data from the NIH CRISP system, adjusted to reflect only expenditures for interferon research, as described in the text.

a. The price deflator used throughout the study is the fixed-weight price index for the gross national product in the *Survey of Current Business,* various issues, table 7-2.

principal investigator (the scientist who is directing the research program), who provides "key words" to be used as descriptors for data retrieval. Independently, a worker in NIH's Division of Research Grants reviews each grant and may assign additional descriptors.

For the current analysis, all awards that could be retrieved from the NIH CRISP data base that used the descriptor *interferon* were evaluated for inclusion in the funding picture.[5] On the basis of project abstracts in the data bases, each award was classified as primary, secondary, or

5. Under the descriptor *interferon* are listed the following subdivisions: interferon inducers, interferon inducers as antineoplastic agents, interferon inducers as antiviral agents, and immunology-interferon.

Figure 3-2. *Extramural Expenditures by the National Institutes of Health for Research in All Biomedical Science, Fiscal Years 1971–81*[a]

**Billions**

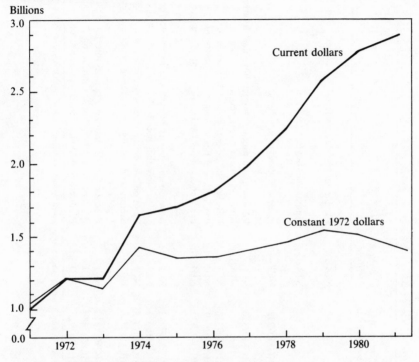

Sources: NIH CRISP reports, 1975–82.
a. Each project devoted at least one-third of the research effort to interferon.

tertiary, according to the percentage of the work effort judged to be interferon related (primary grants were 66 percent interferon related; secondary grants were 33 to 65 percent interferon related; and tertiary grants were less than 33 percent interferon related). All ranking was done solely by the author, to ensure uniform categorization. The grant amounts were then adjusted to reflect the ranking: in other words, a $100,000 grant was counted as $100,000 for a primary ranking, $66,000 for a secondary ranking, and $33,000 for a tertiary ranking. The dollar amounts reflect both direct and indirect costs in 1972 dollars.

INTERFERON FUNDING. Figure 3-1 includes three periods of interferon funding between 1972 and 1982: 1972–75, 1975–78, and 1979–82. While specific developments during each of these periods are discussed in more detail later in the chapter, the general funding pattern may be character-

Table 3-2. *Contracts for Interferon Procurement, 1978–81*

| Purveyor and year | Award amount (dollars) | Contract number | Granting institute | Contract title |
|---|---|---|---|---|
| *1978* | | | | |
| Finnish Red Cross | 300,000 | ... | NIAID[a] | Human leukocyte interferon |
| *1979* | | | | |
| Finnish Red Cross | 500,000 | ... | NIAID | Human leukocyte interferon |
| *1980* | | | | |
| Warner-Lambert Company | 895,000 | 1N01CM07292 | NCI[b] | Human leukocyte interferon |
| Flow Laboratories (subsidiary of Flow General) | 2,071,081 | 1N01CM07370 | NCI | Research and produce human fibroblast interferon |
| Finnish Red Cross | 325,000 | ... | NIAID | Human leukocyte interferon |
| Meloy Laboratories | 989,520 | 1N01CM07378 | NCI | Develop and deliver leukocyte interferon |
| New York Blood Center | 445,843 | 1N01HB02919 | NHLBI[c] | Production of human leukocyte interferon |
| Roswell Park Memorial Institute | 233,441 | 1N01HB02920 | NHLBI | Production of human leukocyte interferon |
| *1981* | | | | |
| Warner-Lambert Company | 37,190 | 3N01CM07292 | NCI | Develop and deliver human leukocyte interferon |
| Meloy Laboratories | 98,653 | 1N01CM15757 | NCI | Collect and distribute biological interferon response modifiers |
| Meloy Laboratories | 56,000 | 3N01CM07378 | NCI | Develop and deliver leukocyte interferon |
| Litton Bionetics | 187,063 | 1N01CM15808 | NCI | Storage and quality assurance of biological response modifiers |
| Meloy Laboratories | 269,973 | 6N01CM15813 | NCI | Produce type II (immune) human interferon |
| Tri-County Health (England) | 2,111,777 | 3N01CM17489 | NCI | Produce human lymphoblast interferon |
| New York Blood Center | 187,389 | 5N01HB02919 | NHLBI | Production of human leukocyte interferon |

Sources: Contracts with numbers were retrieved through the NIH CRISP; those without numbers were procured through a different mechanism and were provided by Maureen W. Myers, NIAID.

a. National Institute of Allergy and Infectious Diseases.
b. National Cancer Institute.
c. National Heart, Lung, and Blood Institute.

ized as follows. During the first period, 1972–75, the eagerness to evaluate interferon by biochemical means lent increasing respectability to the interferon field, but progress was stymied by technological difficulties, as reflected by the decrease in funding during this time from a relative high in 1972. This period was also the time of the early anecdotal stories of interferon's antitumor potential. The second period, 1975–78, is marked by Mathilde Krim's meeting of 1975 and can be viewed as the era of consciousness raising on interferon. Funding gradually increased during these years, with a dramatic increase beginning in 1978, but it still remained below the 1972 level. The third period, 1979–82, a time of sharply rising interferon funding, saw industry's decision to make interferon the demonstration project of commercial biotechnology. These years witnessed an explosion of information about interferon as well as the moderation of hopes about interferon's therapeutic potential. Augmented interferon funding continued until 1980–81, when funds apparently began to decrease. (Adjustment for inflation mitigates the apparent extreme increase in funding beginning in 1979.) Note that while figure 3-1 indicates that expenditures in real dollars for interferon began to decline in 1980–81, an examination of contracts funded during 1978–81 reveals that a large proportion of funds were allocated to procuring interferon for clinical trials (see table 3-2). Most procurement contracts purchased a quantity of interferon to be used for an entire trial's duration. Therefore, the decrease in funds is not a real decline in interferon funding but a reflection of a one-time allocation for materials to be used over several years. In general, the pronounced variance, or year-to-year change, in interferon funding reflects the volatility of interferon funding and possibly the extent to which external factors played a role in funding decisions.

GENERAL BIOMEDICAL RESEARCH FUNDING. The pattern for all biomedical research funding (figure 3-2) is distinctly different from that for interferon funding. First, when funding in constant 1972 dollars is compared, augmented interferon support (1975–82) may be seen to have occurred during a period of stable NIH overall funding for biomedical research. Second, the most dramatic drop in interferon funding (1973–74) took place when overall science funding was increasing in real terms. Figure 3-3 illustrates the differential between the annual relative rates of growth for interferon and those for all science funding for the years 1975 to 1981. The differential was obtained by subtracting the annual relative rate of increase in NIH funding of all scientific research from the same rate of

Figure 3-3. *The Comparative Growth of Research Funding for Interferon and All Biomedical Science, Fiscal Years 1975–81*[a]

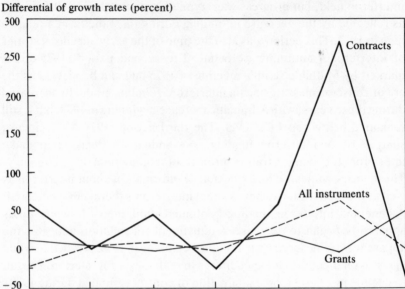

Differential of growth rates (percent)

Sources: Figures 3-1 and 3-2 and table 3-1.
a. The relative change in funding was measured for each year from 1975 through 1981 by calculating differentials. The change in funding for all biomedical research was subtracted from the change in funding for interferon for each year, thereby yielding a measure of the degree to which the growth rate in interferon research funding exceeded the growth rate in biomedical research funding.

increase in interferon funding for each featured year. The differential is also presented for funding by contract or grant mechanism. That there is a positive and substantial differential indicates interferon's relative priority among the NIH's research objectives.

Note that in figures 3-1, 3-2, and 3-3, only extramural program expenditures were analyzed, even though interferon research was also performed under the auspices of the intramural program. Because of cost-accounting procedures at NIH, the author was unable to determine specific allocations for intramural interferon work. Nevertheless, the number of projects within the intramural program directed toward interferon research can be determined (figure 3-4) and follows the same pattern of decline and increase (from fewer than ten projects in 1977 to over forty in 1980) as that for extramural funding. The inclusion of the intramural interferon research dollars would not significantly alter the

Figure 3-4. *Number of NIH Projects for Interferon Research and Production, Fiscal Years 1975–82*[a]

Number

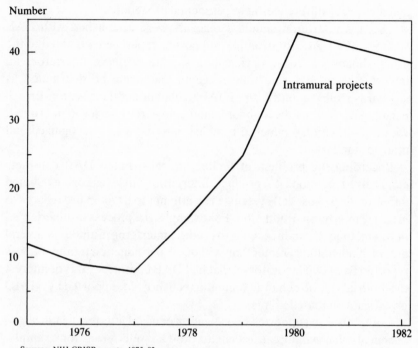

Intramural projects

Sources: NIH CRISP reports, 1975–82.
a. Each project devoted at least one-third of the research effort to interferon.

interferon funding pattern described in this chapter, especially since intramural funds were not spent to procure interferon.

### Early Obstacles to Interferon Development

When the NIH became committed to developing the interferon field, the main scientific roadblocks to progress were problems of standardization, production, and preservation. Contract-funded projects with narrowly defined research aims in these areas were therefore instituted to stimulate the field.

The inability to compare data generated in different laboratories complicated all interferon work. Effective comparison requires a standard method for reporting experimental results. The decision by the NIH to establish reference reagents addressed this problem. (Reference reagents are standard reagents that can be widely distributed. When results from different laboratories are expressed relative to the reference standard, the common reporting system allows direct data comparison and minimizes differences in experimental procedures.)

The first interferon standard reagents were established with DAB support. The DAB, for example, supported experiments that led to the establishment of freeze drying as a way to preserve interferon, an important step in formulating reagents that could be distributed as standards. Subsequently, the NIAID collaborated first with a British panel[6] and, then, as the standards and assays for interferon improved, with a multinational panel to establish internationally recognized and utilized standards.[7]

Regarding the problem of limited supplies, initial DAB contracts emphasized methods to produce interferon. Investigators evaluated different virus–host cell systems in an attempt to develop procedures to increase interferon production. For example, the process of superinduction, a method that induces cells to produce interferon in amounts several orders of magnitude greater than without superinduction treatment, was reported from two laboratories that had DAB contracts.[8] It is of interest that both laboratories had also simultaneously been supported by NIAID investigator-initiated grants.

Contracts also supported investigation of novel interferon inducers—chemicals that would cause cells to produce interferon, for example, synthetic polynucleotides. Preliminary clinical studies with some syn-

6. At a meeting in London in 1969 to determine the development and distribution of interferon reagents, it was decided that the NIAID would undertake development of reference reagents for mouse and rabbit interferons and that the British Medical Research Council (MRC) would take responsibility for human leukocyte interferon standards and chicken interferon standards. This division of responsibility took advantage of the distribution of expertise in the two countries. See "Recommendations of the Conference on Standardization of Interferon and Interferon Inducers," *International Symposium on Interferon and Interferon Inducers*, vol. 14, Symposia Series in Immunobiological Standardization (Basel: S. Karger, 1970), pp. 326–28.

7. See "Interferon Standards: A Memorandum," *Journal of Biological Standardization*, vol. 4, no. 4 (1979), pp. 383–95. A memorandum was drafted on the occasion of an international workshop held at Woodstock, Illinois, in September 1978. The workshop was supported by the National Institute of Allergy and Infectious Diseases, the National Cancer Institute, the Fogarty International Center, and the World Health Organization.

8. E. A. Havell and Jan Vilček, "Production of High-Titered Interferon in Cultures of Human Diploid Cells," *Antimicrobial Agents and Chemotherapy*, vol. 2 (December 1972), pp. 476–84; Y. H. Tan, J. A. Armstrong, and M. Ho, "Accentuation of Interferon Production by Metabolic Inhibitors and its Dependence on Protein Synthesis," *Virology*, vol. 44 (June 1971), pp. 503–09.

thetic inducers showed that they did not effectively induce interferon in man and, what is more, they had the side effect of significant toxicity. Although some contracts were therefore abandoned, other NIAID-funded studies of another interferon inducer, poly IC:LC, are still under clinical assessment.

The DAB also financed conventional interferon production methods by procuring interferon from Dr. Kari Cantell, who, working in Finland, helped greatly to advance the practical production of interferon (see chapter 2). This procurement allowed limited clinical trials to be started in the United States. A small clinical trial had been conducted in England in the early 1970s with Cantell's interferon by Drs. David A. J. Tyrrell and Thomas C. Merigan. When Merigan, who was then on sabbatical leave from Stanford University, returned to California, he purchased interferon from Cantell through the DAB for clinical studies on herpes zoster. The NIAID's policy attempted to support human clinical experimentation as early as possible. To illustrate the various interferon programs supported by NIAID contracts, table 3-3 lists the workscope of 1974 contracts.

A method was also needed to foster rapid communication among workers in the field. Often, empirical experience indicates that a procedure is not going to work or that a line of inquiry is not profitable. Such data are rarely published, although the information is invaluable. Even when information is of publishable quality, the time lag between the submission of a manuscript and its appearance in print may range from several months to several years. The *Interferon Scientific Memoranda,* an NIH-sponsored newsletter containing prepublication, nonrefereed abstracts, attempted to close this information gap. Circulated without cost to investigators who agreed to contribute at least one abstract a year, the *ISM* augmented the information grapevine that operates in any field. Originally established by Dr. Samuel Baron at the NIAID, the *ISM* existed with NIAID support from the mid-1960s until the end of 1981. The DAB viewed its oversight of the *ISM* as an integral part of the interferon program. When budgetary constraints forced the NIAID to abandon support of the publication, funding was undertaken by the Wellcome Foundation as a public service.[9]

The fluctuating patterns of interferon funding seen in figure 3-1

9. The Wellcome Foundation is a British-owned, international group of pharmaceutical and chemical companies including Burroughs Wellcome Company (located in North Carolina) that has had an interest in interferon since the early 1960s.

Table 3-3. *Workscope of NIH-Funded Interferon Contracts, 1974*[a]

| Project number | Award amount (dollars) | Institution | Contract title | Purpose |
|---|---|---|---|---|
| 2N01A102126-05 | 101,394 | Medical College of Pennsylvania | Production of anti-interferon sera (human, mouse) | Research reagent procurement |
| 2N01A102169-07 | 77,369 | New York University | Methods of producing human interferon | Production methods |
| 3N01A122516-06 | 1,306 | Smith Kline & French Laboratories | Purification, safety testing, and preparation of human leukocyte interferon | Quality control |
| 5N01A132529-02 | 81,937 | University of Pittsburgh | Biological stimulators of interferon | Production methods |
| 5N01A132530-03 | 75,001 | Medical College of Wisconsin | Biological stimulators of interferon (bacteria fungi) | Production methods |
| 1N01A142514-00 | 46,749 | Medical College of Wisconsin | Preservation of mammalian interferons as standard reference reagents | Standardization |
| 1N01A142520-00 | 53,598 | Medical College of Wisconsin | Stabilization studies on human interferon | Stabilization |
| 2N01A180654-12 | 35,889 | Aries Corporation Educational Systems | Communication services for interferon investigators | Publication of the *Interferon Scientific Memoranda* |
| 9N01A142527-00 | 87,239 | Stanford University | Evaluate human interferon in disseminated varicella zoster infections | Human evaluation |

Source: Data derived from the NIH CRISP data base.
a. Seven contracts not listed in the table supported the development of animal models to test the efficacy and mechanism of action of antivirals, including interferon.

correlate with the obstacles to progress in interferon research just described. During the period 1972–75, contracts stressed practical problems of production and stabilization, and basic science grants examined mechanisms of interferon's action. Both efforts were hampered by the lack of pure interferon, and by 1975 the information to be gained with the then-current technologies had been nearly exhausted.

### New Developments

The year 1975 marks the beginning of a second period of interferon funding, from 1975 to 1978, which is characterized by relatively stable, though low, funding. Simultaneously, fundamental advances in biochemical genetics made feasible the use of genetic engineering techniques to isolate and manufacture scarce proteins like interferon. The Sloan-Kettering Institute conference organized by Mathilde Krim, results from Hans Strander's experiments, and lobbying for interferon as a potential cancer treatment also occurred in this period. These events, combined with the technological revolution, resulted in a dramatic upswing in funding for the third period, 1979–82.

### Comparing NCI and NIAID Funding

Although Galasso and the NIAID's DAB have been the most consistently vocal proponents for interferon studies at the NIH, the National Cancer Institute has historically expended more funds than the NIAID for interferon research. From 1972 to 1982 the NIH provided funding for a total of 1,535 intramural and extramural interferon projects, with the NCI funding 628 of these and the NIAID 542. Because these two institutes account for the bulk of NIH involvement in interferon research, the present discussion focuses on their activities.[10]

Although the NCI contribution in absolute dollars was greater than the NIAID's (figure 3-5), the latter's contribution represents a larger

10. Other NIH institutes contributing resources for interferon research during 1972–82 included: National Institutes on Aging (seven projects); Arthritis, Diabetes, and Digestive and Kidney Diseases (seventy-eight projects); Dental Research (twenty-one projects); Environmental Health Sciences (twenty-one projects); General Medical Sciences (thirty-eight projects); Child Health and Human Development (twenty projects); Heart, Lung, and Blood Diseases (thirteen projects); Neurological and Communicative Disorders and Stroke (thirty-nine projects); and the Eye Institute (sixty-five projects).

Figure 3-5. *Comparison of Extramural Research Expenditures
for Interferon with Those for All Biomedical Science, National Cancer
Institute and National Institute for Allergy and Infectious Diseases,
Fiscal Years 1971–82*[a]

Millions of 1972 dollars

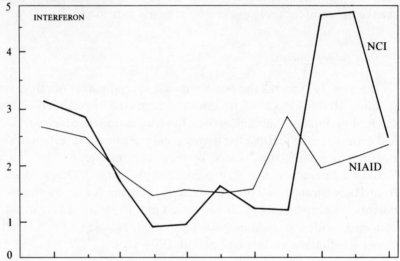

Millions of 1972 dollars

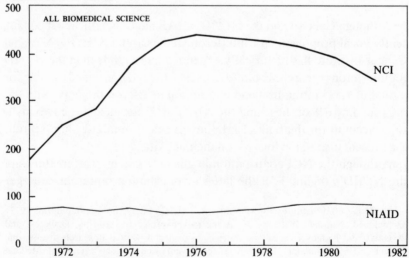

Sources: NIH CRISP reports and *NIH Data Book, 1982.*
a. Includes all types of funding mechanisms.

proportion of its research budget, indicating the high priority it placed on interferon. Between 1972 and 1981 the NIAID spent between 2.0 and 3.5 percent of its annual research budget on interferon. In contrast, during this period the NCI annually spent between 0.15 and 1.30 percent of its budget for this purpose. Just as the NIH spending effort for interferon was different from the funding in other areas of science (figure 3-1), the patterns of interferon support within both NCI and the NIAID were totally unlike the distribution of overall research funded by each institute (figure 3-5).

As pointed out earlier, the NIAID antiviral substances program had been formed to investigate interferon as an antiviral agent. As may be seen by comparing figures 3-1 and 3-5, in the early 1970s the NIAID distributed a large proportion of the total NIH interferon funds. Although interferon's antitumor potential was not seriously considered in the United States until the mid-1970s, the NCI's early efforts in interferon can be explained by its interest in viruses.

The National Cancer Act of 1971 had targeted research on "viruses which might cause cancer."[11] It was natural to look not only for tumor viruses but also for antiviral agents. Therefore, NCI funds for interferon decreased in the mid-1970s for the same reason that NIAID funds declined; that is, technical limits for exploring interferon's antiviral properties had been reached. During the late 1970s, the antiviral potential of interferon remained the NIAID's primary interest in it. In the late 1970s, however, the NCI became interested in antitumor properties of interferon that did not hinge on the protein's antiviral effects. The NCI's substantial expenditures for interferon in the late 1970s can be traced to hopes for interferon's antitumor potential as a regulator of the immune response, also known as its "biological-response-modifying" activity. In 1978, in response to growing congressional pressure for answers on interferon, the NCI formalized its interferon program and named it the biological response modifiers program. Although the BRMP charter stipulates substances in addition to interferon,[12] during fiscal year 1981 approximately 80 percent of BRMP funds were spent on interferon.

11. 85 Stat. 778.

12. The BRMP, a comprehensive program of the NCI's Division of Cancer Treatment (DCT), is involved in clinical and laboratory research with both extramural and intramural components to investigate, develop, and bring to clinical trials potential therapeutic agents that may alter biological responses important in the biology of cancer growth and metastasis. The classes of agents to be investigated in this program include immunoaugmenting, immunomodulating, and immunorestorative agents, interferons and

*Use of Funding Instruments*

The distinctive interferon funding curves of the NIH, the NCI, and the NIAID are due to increases in both targeted and nontargeted research expenditures, as illustrated by comparing the contract and grant funding for interferon research with equivalent data for overall biomedical research (figure 3-6).

Between 1978 and 1981 money was expended for interferon research at a rate that vastly outpaced the growth for overall biomedical science research. From 1978 to 1982 the number of interferon grants increased by 58 percent, while the total number of science research grants increased by only 22 percent.

Although no legislation specifically relating to interferon was introduced between 1979 and 1982, interferon figured prominently in several congressional hearings. At 1979 hearings before the Senate Committee on Appropriations, the directors of the NCI and the NIAID, Dr. Arthur C. Upton and Dr. Richard M. Krause, respectively, responded to questions on progress in interferon research and emphasized their intention to pursue efforts in this area.[13] The subsequent committee report recommended that a substantial portion of the increase in the NCI's annual budget be devoted to interferon research and that funding might be used "to develop the methods to identify, purify, and manufacture these materials for clinical tests."[14] Finally, the report asked that the NCI develop within thirty days of passage of the appropriations bill a plan that it would send to the committee, detailing its funding intentions for interferon and describing actions being taken to coordinate efforts with the NIAID. In the corresponding hearings in the House of Representatives, interferon was also mentioned in the Appropriations staff report, but as was true with the Senate committee, no dollar figure was

---

interferon inducers, lymphokines, cytokines, antigrowth factors, thymic factors, tumor antigens and modifiers of tumor antigens on cell membranes, antitumor antibodies, antitumor cells, and maturation and differentiation factors. Robert K. Oldham, "Biological Response Modifiers Program," *Journal of Biological Response Modifiers*, vol. 1, no. 1 (1982), pp. 81–100.

13. Statements of Arthur C. Upton and Richard M. Krause in *Departments of Labor and Health, Education and Welfare and Related Agencies Appropriations, Fiscal Year 1980*, Hearings before the Senate Committee on Appropriations, 96 Cong. 1 sess. (Government Printing Office, 1979), pt. 1, pp. 350, 531–32.

14. *Departments of Labor and Health, Education and Welfare, and Related Agencies Appropriation Bill, 1980*, S. Rept. 96-247, 96 Cong. 1 sess. (GPO, 1979), p. 47.

Figure 3-6.  *Comparison of NIH Grant and Contract Expenditures for Research on Interferon with Those for All Biomedical Science, Fiscal Years 1971–82*[a]

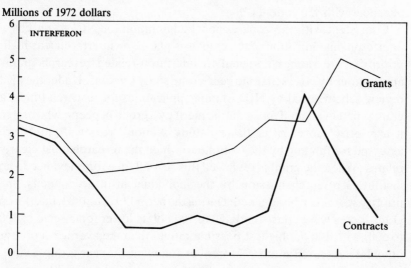

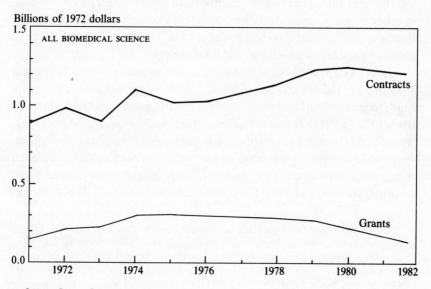

Sources: Same as figure 3-5.
a. See table 3-1 for the definition of grants and contracts.

specified for interferon research expenditure.[15] In Senate appropriations hearings held in 1980, however, the NCI proposed that $8 million to $9 million be used to purchase interferon for clinical trials on a dozen kinds of cancer with 450 patients.[16]

Consistent with the congressional admonition for NCI to purchase interferon, an indication of the emphasis placed on interferon was high-priority score ratings assigned to interferon-related research grants applications by NIH scientific peer-group study sections. Under the dual review scheme used by NIH to rank applications for research funds, a grant is first evaluated for scientific merit by a group of peers, who assign it a priority score. After these "study section" reviews, grants are assessed for funding by the institute to which the research most clearly relates. When the grant is reviewed this second time for relevance to an institute's research mission by the individual institute councils, the priority scores can be adjusted. During the period 1972 to 1982, interferon grant scores were consistently 50 to 100 points lower (on a scale of 100 to 500, with 100 the highest possible rating) than the average score for other NIH research grants.[17] Moreover, following the peer-group review, interferon grant scores were not adjusted any more frequently than those in other areas by councils within the NIH institutes themselves. Therefore, the feeling that interferon was a "hot" area was shared by both groups of scientists who reviewed for the NIH.

The NIAID and the NCI used grants and contracts differently (figures 3-7 and 3-8). The NIAID consistently devoted a greater proportion of its funds to grants than to contracts in both interferon and all science funding from 1971 to 1982. In overall science funding, the NCI used contracts with nearly the same intensity as grants from 1971 until the mid-1970s. After 1975 the NCI channeled an increasing amount of funds through the grant mechanism, most probably in response to criticism of the institute's general abuse of the contract mechanism.[18] The criticism

15. *Departments of Labor and Health, Education and Welfare, and Related Agencies Appropriation Bill, 1980*, H. Rept. 96-244, 96 Cong. 1 sess. (GPO, 1979), p. 30.

16. *Departments of Labor and Health, Education and Welfare and Related Agencies Appropriations for Fiscal Year 1981*, Hearings before the Senate Committee on Appropriations, 96 Cong. 2 sess. (GPO, 1980), pt. 1, pp. 721–22.

17. Figures are based on averaging of priority scores of interferon and all science research grants with R01, R22, R23, and P01 classifications that were funded for each year from 1972 to 1982.

18. See discussion of NCI contracts in the report of the Ad Hoc Committee to Review the National Cancer Plan. Dr. Lewis Thomas, "The National Cancer Program

Figure 3-7. *Comparison of NIAID Grant and Contract Expenditures for Research on Interferon with Those for All Biomedical Science, Fiscal Years 1971–82*[a]

Millions of 1972 dollars

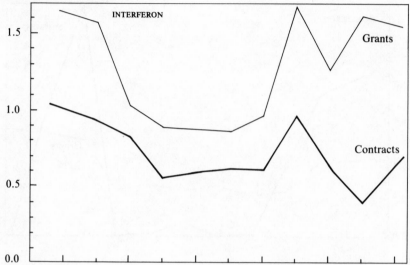

Millions of 1972 dollars

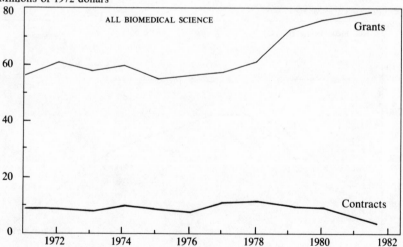

Sources: Same as figure 3-5.
a. See table 3-1 for the definition of grants and contracts.

Figure 3-8. *Comparison of NCI Grant and Contract Expenditures for Research on Interferon with Those for All Biomedical Science, Fiscal Years 1971–82*[a]

Millions of 1972 dollars

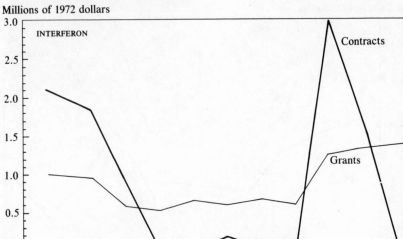

Millions of 1972 dollars

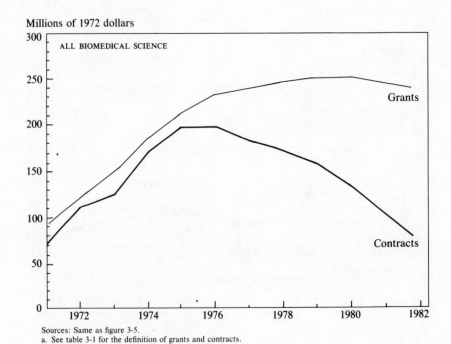

Sources: Same as figure 3-5.
a. See table 3-1 for the definition of grants and contracts.

Figure 3-9. *Average NIH Contract Award Level for Research on Interferon and for All Biomedical Science Research, Fiscal Years 1971–81*[a]

Thousands of 1972 dollars

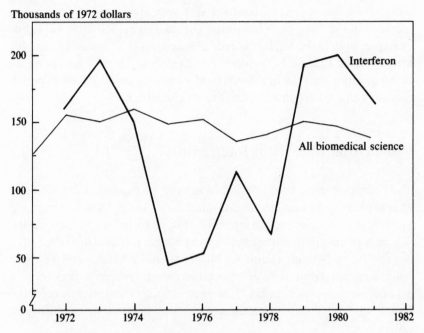

Sources: Same as figure 3-5.
a. Award amounts were not adjusted to reflect the proportion of research that was interferon related, so that the data can be compared with the average size of contract awards in all biomedical science.

centered on the awarding of NCI contracts outside the traditional peer review system, in addition to the allegation that funds were diverted to favored individuals and programs at the expense of peer-reviewed grants. In light of this criticism, the NCI decision to use contracts for interferon may be seen to represent a decision that contracts are an effective mechanism for achieving research goals. In contrast, the NCI's spending for interferon grants remained relatively stable throughout the 1971–82 period.

The average award size is another measure of targeting funding. The average award level for individual grants and contracts remained relatively constant for overall science grants during 1971–81 (see figure 3-9).

Plan: A Review" (Washington, D.C.: National Academy of Sciences, 1973); and Vincent T. DeVita, Jr., "The Governance of Science at the National Cancer Institute: A Perspective on Misperceptions," *Cancer Research,* vol. 43 (August 1983), pp. 3969–73.

In contrast, the size of interferon contracts fluctuated in a pattern similar to that for interferon funding in figure 3-1. As seen in the figure, contracts were larger in times of major procurement initiatives (1979–81). The increase in the interferon contract size was also accompanied by an increase in the number of interferon contracts awarded after 1979. For example, in 1978 the NIH awarded 2,030 contracts, of which 10 were for interferon. In 1980, of 1,560 contracts, 20 were for interferon. There can be no question that the interferon field was stimulated by NIH expenditures and that both contracts and grants contributed.

## Industrial Interest in Interferon

Although commercial interest in interferon expanded dramatically after the meeting organized by Mathilde Krim in 1975 and its follow-up in 1979, industrial interest in interferon can be traced to the early 1960s. A long-term commitment to interferon by pharmaceutical manufacturers began first in Britain. Derek C. Burke, then a postdoctoral fellow in Alick Isaacs's laboratory and now director of research at Allelix, a genetic boutique in Canada, has been a long-time interferonologist. Recalling the British pharmaceutical industry's entry into interferon, he noted:

> Although basic virology was then very primitive, interferon was perceived as a potential antiviral. In 1959 a committee was set up which involved the Medical Research Council, Imperial Chemical Industries [ICI], Wellcome, and Glaxo[19] to try to develop interferon as an antibiotic. Lying hard on people then was the history of penicillin, discovered in Britain but ultimately developed in the U.S.A. Fees were paid to U.S. firms who had received patents, and that has never been forgotten. That's one of the reasons that in Britain the biomedical scientists are under pressure to patent.[20]
>
> Isaacs was chairman of the committee and in his enthusiasm oversold interferon. What we [had] with cancer in the late seventies happened [with]

19. This is a good model of government-academe-industry affiliation in Britain. The Medical Research Council (MRC) is a government institution, in some ways analogous to the NIH. ICI, the Wellcome Foundation, and Glaxo Holdings are pharmaceutical houses.

20. Alick Isaacs and Jean Lindenmann filed their first application for a patent on interferon in Germany on March 11, 1958, and their first application for a U.S. patent on May 9, 1958 (serial #734,106). U.S. Patent #3,699,222, issued on October 17, 1972, was entitled "Production of Viral Interfering Substances," claiming "1. Interferon, 2. Human Interferon, 3. Monkey Interferon, 4. Chick Interferon."

viruses in the early sixties. In the middle sixties the drug companies got disillusioned. ICI and Glaxo spent a lot of money and got nothing out of it. They pulled out and only Wellcome stayed in. People who had been working on interferon at the other firms landed up at Wellcome. Even they became disillusioned because we just didn't make enough interferon.

In the United States industrial interest in interferon was limited during the 1960s, although some effort was directed toward exploring interferon and interferon inducers at Merck, Sharpe and Dohme Research Laboratories; Schering-Plough Corporation; Smith Kline & French Laboratories; and E. I. du Pont de Nemours & Company. By the early 1970s, owing to technical limitations on the production of interferon, Schering-Plough and Smith Kline and French, as well as the British ICI and Glaxo, abandoned interferon. Yet the pharmaceutical market's continuing need for antiviral therapies stimulated renewed interest in interferon by industry when, by the mid-1970s, technical innovations in interferon production and purification were developed. Industry's interest was heightened all the more by the publicity accorded Krim's meetings, which highlighted interferon's potential as an antitumor agent and recognized the need to test the emerging genetic engineering technology.

## The Role of Consciousness Raising

Mathilde Krim's 1975 and 1979 meetings have already been mentioned as important consciousness raisers in the interferon effort. Several anecdotes further illustrate the importance of consciousness raising in industry's decision to choose interferon as a demonstration project of genetic engineering technology.

In 1980 Meloy Laboratories, a subsidiary of the Revlon Health Care Group, won an NCI contract[21] to produce interferon-alpha. Meloy's decision to produce interferon resulted from the enthusiasm of several members of Revlon's board of directors, who argued that if interferon was truly a wonder drug, Meloy needed interferon in order to be a competitive pharmaceutical company. To implement an interferon program, Meloy had not only recruited several young scientists, including one with experience in interferon, but had also built a facility for the sterile production and packaging of Cantell-type interferon. Asked why

21. Contract #1N01CM07378 awarded $989,520 to Meloy Laboratories for research process development and delivery of 50 billion units of leukocyte interferon (Cantell interferon-alpha).

Table 3-4. *U.S. Industrial Interferon Effort, Pharmaceutical Houses, 1982*

| Company | Ownership | Involvement in interferon |
|---|---|---|
| Bristol-Myers Company, New York, New York[a] | Public corporation | Holds exclusive worldwide license to use and sell interferon manufactured using Genex Corporation technology and to use and sell interferon purchased from Interferon Sciences in 1981. |
| Burroughs Wellcome Company, Research Triangle Park, North Carolina[b,c] | Privately held by Wellcome Foundation, United Kingdom | Manufactures "Wellferon," an interferon-alpha preparation. Interferon research and clinical trials performed in the United Kingdom and the United States. Most production is in the United Kingdom. |
| E. I. du Pont de Nemours & Company, Wilmington, Delaware[b,d] | Public corporation | In-house research since mid-1960s. Tissue culture and recombinant-DNA techniques to produce interferon-beta on a laboratory scale. |
| G. D. Searle & Company, Chicago, Illinois[b,d] | Public corporation | Researches and produces in the United Kingdom interferon-beta, interferon-gamma, and hybrid interferons using recombinant-DNA techniques. Planned to enter clinical trials by the end of 1983. |
| Hoffmann-La Roche, Nutley, New Jersey[c,d] | Privately held subsidiary of Hoffmann-La Roche and Company, Basel, Switzerland | Interferon research since 1969 performed by the Roche Institute of Molecular Biology. Producing recombinant interferon-alpha originally cloned by Genentech. Also involved in in-house research in interferon-beta and interferon-gamma. |
| Schering-Plough Corporation, Kenilworth, New Jersey[e] | Public corporation | Owns 8 percent equity in Biogen S.A. and is producing Biogen recombinant interferon-alpha. Also involved in in-house research on interferon-gamma. |
| Upjohn Company, Kalamazoo, Michigan[b,d] | Public corporation | In-house interferon research. Produces Puraminadadone, a human and animal interferon inducer. |

a. Company annual report or prospectus.
b. *Telegen Directory of U.S. Biotechnology* (New York: EIC Intelligence, 1983).
c. *Genetic Engineering News*, vol. 2 (November–December 1982), pp. 6–19.
d. Direct discussion with corporation.
e. *Biotechnology U.S.A. March 1982* (London: IMS World Publications, 1982).

the NCI would write a procurement contract with a company that had not yet demonstrated the ability to generate the product, one interferonologist conjectured about those events.

> At that point, nobody had the demonstrated ability to make interferon other than Kari Cantell, and NCI wanted to have interferon producers in the States. When something is established, it's reasonable to have track records, and that weighs heavily in the decision to award contracts. I think the NIH was confronted with a tremendous political push from downtown saying, "We're putting money into the budget this year for interferon. Why aren't you guys spending?"[22]

> The contract was initiated in 1980 and ran for about eighteen months and Meloy never delivered any interferon [owing to technical problems]. Eventually some was made and the upshot is that Revlon got stuck with an inventory of about $700,000 of alpha-interferon. This was a straight loss because by that time recombinant alpha-interferon came up.

> Then the decision was made to go into gamma-interferon. Revlon had a government contract which had to do with gamma-interferon. If you look at the total amount of money that Revlon has invested in interferon (including building a facility) relative to what the government has invested in contracts, the government has gotten a tremendous free ride. All developmental costs were essentially borne by Revlon, although the government thinks it has underwritten the cost of developing gamma-interferon.[23]

Meloy was not the only company whose interferon production was fostered by the interest of its executive officers. Ronald E. Cape, former chairman and chief executive officer of Cetus Corporation, had a difficult time raising capital in the early 1980s. As a result of the interest of a Shell Oil Company executive, Cetus and Shell established a partnership, with Shell providing $30 million earmarked for interferon R&D. Similarly, in 1980 the chairman of the board of Bristol-Myers Company initiated what led to a contract for interferon production with Genex Corporation.

## Problems of Interferon as a Demonstration Project

The two kinds of companies active in genetic engineering and interferon R&D have been divisions of large pharmaceutical companies and new genetic boutiques (tables 3-4 and 3-5). Choosing interferon as a

22. See the discussion earlier in this chapter, "Use of Funding Instruments."

23. Government expenditures for industrial development of interferon in the form of procurement contracts for 1978–81 are shown in table 3-2. The hidden federal investment in industry—providing reference reagents, the *Interferon Scientific Memoranda*, and consensus conferences—should also be noted (see table 3-3). Specific dollar figures for Revlon's investment in interferon-gamma are proprietary information. Table 3-6 lists minimal estimates for genetically engineered interferon.

Table 3-5. *U.S. Industrial Interferon Effort, Genetic Boutiques, 1983*

| Company | Date of incorporation | Ownership | Measure of corporate size[a] | Type of interferon produced or researched[b] |
|---|---|---|---|---|
| Advanced Biotechnologies, Silver Spring, Maryland[c,d] | February 1982 | Privately held | 7 employees | Lymphoblastoid, gamma |
| Applied Molecular Genetics (Amgen), Newbury Park, California[d,e,f] | April 1980 | Privately held; filed for a first public offering July 1983 | 100 employees, 45 Ph.D.s; March 1983 total assets, $11.5 million; March 1983 total equity, $10.1 million; current ratio, 4.3 | Alpha "analog," gamma |
| Bioassay Systems Corporation, Woburn, Massachusetts[d,e] | 1977 | Privately held; 80 percent owned by Pedco Group | 60 employees, 12 Ph.D.s; projected 1982 revenues, $3 million | All human and animal |
| Biogen, Cambridge, Massachusetts[e] | 1978 | Public corporation since March 1983; wholly owned by Biogen S.A., a Swiss corporation | 70 employees, 22 Ph.D.s; financial data on American division not available | All human and animal |
| Biotech Research Laboratories, Rockville, Maryland[c,f,g] | March 1973 | Public corporation since March 1981 | 1982 total assets, $5.6 million; stockholders' equity, $4.2 million; current ratio, 9.0 | Beta |
| Cetus Corporation, Berkeley, California[d,f] | March 1971 | Public corporation since March 1981 | 1982 total assets, $132.6 million; stockholders' equity, $128.3 million; current ratio, 25.7 | Alpha, beta |
| Collaborative Research, Lexington, Massachusetts[e,f] | September 1961 | Public corporation since February 1982 | 140 employees; 1982 total assets, $20.5 million; stockholders' equity, $18.8 million; current ratio, 12.0 | Alpha, beta |

| Company, Location | Date | Corporate status | Financial data | Interferon types |
|---|---|---|---|---|
| Cooper Vision, Palo Alto, California[d,f,g] | July 1961 | Wholly owned by Cooper Laboratories, a public corporation | Financial data available for parent corporation only | Alpha |
| Damon Biotech, Needham Heights, Massachusetts[c,d,e] | 1980 | A division of Damon Corporation, a public corporation | 40 employees, 10 Ph.D.s; 1982 total assets, $95.1 million; stockholders' equity, $39.3 million; current ratio, 3.0 | n.a. |
| Electro-Nucleonics Laboratories, Silver Spring, Maryland[d,h] | 1969 | Public corporation; merged with parent company, Electro-Nucleonics, July 1983 | 700 employees; 1982 total assets, $33.6 million; stockholders' equity, $93,884; current ratio, 2.0 | Alpha, beta, gamma |
| Enzo Biochem, New York, New York[e,f] | 1976 | Public corporation since June 1980 | 40 employees, 20 Ph.D.s; 1982 total assets, $17.8 million; stockholders' equity, $16.1 million; current ratio, 46.0 | Enzoferon, a topical preparation of interferon-alpha, currently undergoing clinical trials |
| Flow General, McLean, Virginia[d,g] | Interferon research since 1978 | Public corporation | 1982 total assets, $194.3 million; stockholders' equity, $94.7 million; current ratio, 2.2 | Beta, gamma |
| Genentech, South San Francisco, California[f] | April 1976 | Public corporation since October 1980 | 450 employees, 90 Ph.D.s; 1982 total assets, $101.2 million; stockholders' equity, $84.3 million; current ratio, 4.9 | All human and bovine leukocyte |
| Genetics Institute, Boston, Massachusetts[d,e] | December 1980 | Privately held | 35 employees, 10 senior scientists | Gamma |
| Genex Corporation, Rockville, Maryland[e,f] | July 1977 | Public corporation since September 1982 | 200 employees, 50 Ph.D.s; total assets, $31.8 million; stockholders' equity, $26.8 million; current ratio, 5.6 | Alpha, beta |

Table 3-5 (*continued*)

| Company | Date of incorporation | Ownership | Measure of corporate size[a] | Type of interferon produced or researched[b] |
|---|---|---|---|---|
| Hem Research, Rockville, Maryland[d,e] | 1966 | Privately held | 50 employees, 6 Ph.D.s | Beta |
| Interferon Sciences, New Brunswick, New Jersey[c-g] | January 1980 | Public corporation since May 1981; 75 percent owned by the National Patent Development Corporation | 20 employees; 1982 total assets, $8.4 million; stockholders' equity, $8.4 million; current ratio, 10.5 | Alpha, gamma |
| Lee BioMolecular Research Labs, San Diego, California[d,e] | August 1980 | Privately held | 10 employees, 2 Ph.D.s | Human and animal (rabbit and mouse) |
| Life Sciences, Inc., St. Petersburg, Florida[c,f] | 1962; research in interferon-alpha since 1979 | Public corporation since 1968 | 48 employees; 1982 total assets, $1.3 million; stockholders' equity, $856,890; current ratio, 2.1 | Alpha |
| Meloy Labs, Springfield, Virginia[d,e] | 1970; research in interferon-alpha since 1979 | Wholly owned subsidiary of Revlon, a public corporation | 400 employees, 22 Ph.D.s | Alpha, beta |
| National Geno Sciences, Southfield, Michigan[d,e] | May 1979 | Privately held | 30 employees, 7 Ph.D.s | Alpha, gamma |
| New England Enzyme Center, Boston, Massachusetts[d,e] | September 1963; interferon research contract from 1980 to 1981 | Part of Tufts University School of Medicine | 12 employees, 5 Ph.D.s | Alpha, beta |

| Company | Date | Corporate status | Financial/employee data | Interferon type |
| --- | --- | --- | --- | --- |
| North American Biologicals, Miami, Florida[c,d,f] | March 1968 | Public corporation since April 1969 | 1982 total stockholders' equity, $1.3 million; current ratio, 0.93 | Alpha |
| Serono Laboratories, Randolph, Massachusetts[d,e] | 1977 | Privately held by Swiss-based ARES Applied Research Systems N.V. | 83 employees | Beta |
| Southern Biotech, Brandon, Florida[c,d] | Biotechnology activities since 1981; filed Chapter Eleven on May 28, 1982 | Public corporation | 15 employees | Alpha |
| Viragen, Miami, Florida[d,e] | December 1980 | Public corporation; 69 percent owned by Automated Medical Labs | 7 employees; 1981 total assets, $274,267; stockholders' equity, $37,967 | Alpha (plans for gamma) |

n.a. Not available.
a. Unless otherwise stated, estimates of company valuation are as of January 1983. The current ratio is current assets divided by current liability.
b. All interferons listed are human unless otherwise noted.
c. *Genetic Engineering News*, vol. 2 (November–December 1982), pp. 6–19.
d. Direct discussion with corporation.
e. *Telegen Directory of U.S. Biotechnology* (New York: EIC Intelligence, 1983).
f. Company annual report or prospectus.
g. *Biotechnology U.S.A.*, *March 1982* (London: IMS World Publications, 1982).
h. *IMS Pharmaceutical Marketletter*, January 3, 1983, p. 9.

demonstration project has involved much greater risk for genetic boutiques than for the larger companies. The large houses already had
pharmaceutical development and distribution facilities, including experience with product scale-up and with regulatory and clinical trial
processes. The decision of such corporations to work on interferon
hardly constituted a threat to their well-being, especially since interferon
was only a small percentage of their total research effort. But for
companies with only genetic engineering expertise, selecting interferon
was a different matter. If these boutiques were to provide discovery
work services only, they needed to establish appropriate collaborative
arrangements with other corporations. Furthermore, if they intended to
produce the product themselves (as did Southern Biotech and Biotechnologies), the risk of failure was high. The following table shows some
interferon-related joint ventures in the United States.

| New genetic engineering company | Established corporate partner |
|---|---|
| Biogen | Schering-Plough Corporation |
| Cetus Corporation | Shell Oil Company |
| Genentech | Hoffmann-La Roche |
| Genex Corporation | Bristol-Myers Company |
| Interferon Sciences | Bristol-Myers Company, Anheuser-Busch Companies, and Collaborative Research Corporation |

The long period between product development and sale of pharmaceuticals, as well as the cost and uncertainty of clinical trials, makes the
development of any pharmaceutical a long-term, costly, and high-risk
endeavor. This is especially true for the test of a new technology. Table
3-6 delineates the stages in the development of a genetically engineered
interferon and the estimated minimum time and minimum costs required
to complete each stage. These estimates were made after evaluating the
experiences of several companies (Meloy, Schering-Plough, and Cetus)
in developing interferon-alpha and interferon-gamma. The estimated
costs in the table are based on the assumption that the appropriate capital
equipment and work site are available. J. Allan Waitz, president of
DNAX Research Institute, the genetic engineering subsidiary of Schering-Plough, estimates that if such facilities need to be built, the cost of
equipping and modifying laboratories for fermentation and purification
would involve tens of thousands of dollars, requiring two to six months

for a facility that could produce interferon in quantities needed for research. For a pilot plant, Waitz estimates that $500,000 to $3,000,000 would be required and would take twelve to eighteen months; and for a commercial production plant tens of millions of dollars would be spent over an eighteen- to thirty-five-month period.[24]

Cetus Corporation is the oldest genetic engineering concern in the United States. When asked about the outlook for the many genetic boutiques, Cetus's first president and chief operating officer, Peter J. Farley, commented: "The vast majority are either going to go belly-up or be picked up by large companies. The reason is that this is expensive research and most companies have not raised enough money to make it through more than one or at most two years. Most of them cannot conceivably produce products in that period of time to provide revenue."

## The Fascination with a Cancer Cure

Farley's observations are as true for boutiques owned by large corporations as for those that were the first ventures of professor-entrepreneurs. The costs of bringing a human pharmaceutical to market are well known, and new boutiques might have been more wisely counseled to concentrate on products geared to the fine chemical, veterinary, or agricultural markets, because the sale of these does not necessitate the lengthy approval process that is required for human pharmaceuticals. Certainly some small start-up firms must have been formed under the assumption that once they had demonstrated competence in discovery work they would quickly be bought out by a larger corporation; such a strategy would not require a boutique to generate capital to cover all phases. Nevertheless, Cetus's decision to capitalize on what it saw as the "green-light" aspect of anticancer work may be more typical. Farley stated:

> We said we'd concentrate on things that could be commercialized in a reasonable period of time. Diagnostics is one area, and indeed, these can be very free of regulations. Delay is often less than one year, and we'll market our first diagnostic in November 1982.[25] We'll concentrate in two areas,

24. Comments from personal interviews; also a presentation by J. Allan Waitz, "Interferon: A Demonstration Project for the Commercial Application of Genetic Engineering," paper presented at the annual meeting of the American Association for the Advancement of Science, Detroit, Michigan, May 27, 1983.

25. As of December 1982, Cetus Corp. was receiving royalties for a monoclonal antibody marketed by Cappel Laboratories for use in diagnosing low-back pain.

Table 3-6. *Development of Genetically Engineered Interferons*[a]

| Phase | Workscope | Minimal estimated time (years) | Minimal estimated cost (dollars)[a] |
|---|---|---|---|
| Discovery | Gene cloning<br>Identification and isolation of gene<br>Insertion of gene into vector<br>Expression of interferon in<br>  microorganism or yeast | 1 | 2 million |
| Development phase<br>  Preclinical | Expansion to production volumes<br>Pilot plant production<br>Assay and scale up (requires new<br>  techniques)<br>Purification (requires new techniques)<br>Manufacture for preclinical tests<br>Toxicity and safety testing in animals<br>Efficacy tests in animals *in vivo*<br>Award investigational new drug (IND)<br>  certification for clinical trials | 2–4 | 2 million |
|   Clinical | Clinical trials<br><br>Toxicity and safety trials<br>Phase one<br>Phase two<br>Phase three | 2–5 | 10s of millions |

Sources: Composite of remarks by executives at Meloy Laboratories, Schering-Plough Corporation, and Cetus Corporation.

a. Cost estimate assumes that facilities are already in place and that major capital equipment is not needed. The estimates also assume that the knowledge gained from the first successful "cloning" of an interferon is available at the time the discovery phase work is begun.

infectious diseases and cancer. The second area is in therapeutics. If you go for products that people will take long term, they'll take one pill a day for the rest of their lives—an antiarthritic or antihypertensive, for example—then long-term toxicity and efficacy trials can drag things out seven to ten years. But we have purposely concentrated on anticancer therapeutics, and there's a good businesslike, regulatory reason. If a new compound appears worthwhile, you can get it into the marketplace quicker if it's an anticancer compound. Recently, one company got an anticancer compound through the FDA in two and one-half years. The reasons are obvious. The compounds are meant to treat people who are terminally ill and for whom other things haven't worked. There's very little reason to run seven-, eight-, or ten-year toxicity tests. The risk-benefit is so enormous that [regulatory agencies] can shorten the time cycle.

Farley's contention that the regulatory cycle can be altered for cancer drugs is substantiated at the state level. In 1982 the Florida legislature passed two laws allowing practitioners to use unconventional therapies in the control of cancer even though the drugs may not have received investigational new drug or new drug application approval from the

FDA. The laws, known as the Cancer Therapeutic Research Act of 1981 and the Drug Device Cosmetic Act Revision of 1981, created a technical review panel appointed by the secretary of the Florida Health and Rehabilitative Services that establishes protocols and grants approval for use of a new drug.[26] As of May 1983 the only applications filed under these laws have been for the use of interferon, and three are pending approval. A similar law has been passed in Oklahoma and another is under consideration in Pennsylvania. Interferon's lure as an anticancer agent cannot be discounted in the drive to develop interferon commercially. Susan Sontag, in *Illness as Metaphor,* has expounded on the aberrant fear the modern world has of cancer.[27] The fascination of a cancer cure drove researchers, investors, and the business community to target interferon.

In the early 1980s the Wall Street firm of E. F. Hutton conducted a short-lived experiment to form a mutual fund for biotechnology venture capital investment, called DNA Sciences. Dr. Zsolt Harsanyi, a geneticist and former staff member at the Congressional Office of Technology Assessment, was named president of DNA Sciences, which seriously considered and then decided against financing a widely publicized genetic boutique in Israel that was to produce and research interferon. Harsanyi contends that interferon was the catalyst for public investment in biotechnology and that the cancer-cure mystique of interferon was invaluable in mobilizing venture capital for biotechnology.

Supporting this impression are the results of a survey of industrialists interested in interferon, conducted by a market research firm at the First International Interferon Congress, held in Washington, D.C., in 1980.[28] Registrants were polled for their knowledge about interferon and its promise, their speculations on the future of interferon, and the resources that would be required to bring interferon to market. Survey responses indicate the kind of information that was then available to companies to enable them to decide whether to pursue interferon R&D. On average, 50 percent of respondents answered "Don't know" when queried about

26. Cancer Therapeutic Research Act of 1981, *Florida Statutes Annotated,* sec. 402.36; and the 1981 amendment to the Florida Food, Drug, and Cosmetic Act, *Florida Statutes Annotated,* sec. 500.01 et seq.

27. Susan Sontag, *Illness as Metaphor* (Farrar, Strauss, & Giroux, 1978).

28. *Interferon Forum '81,* Technology Marketing Group Report 124 (Des Plaines, Ill.: The Group, 1980). The First International Interferon Congress was itself an indication of the growth of commercial interest in interferon: the congress was organized by Scherago Associates and the publishers of the *Journal of Interferon Research* in part to publicize the inauguration of the journal.

interferon's efficacy for treating fifteen different cancers and viral diseases. Yet 46 percent of ninety respondents reported that they were involved in planning for interferon production, and 70 percent of thirty-seven respondents were already engaged in interferon pilot programs.[29]

### Boutique Successes and Failures

The prominence of interferon as a demonstration project for young boutiques is evident in table 3-5. Of the twenty-six boutiques listed in the table, only ten were founded before 1976. In addition, interferon figured prominently in the stock prospectuses and annual reports of the seventeen publicly held boutiques.

The boutiques cited in the table may be divided naturally on the basis of capitalization. Several boutiques (Genentech, Cetus Corporation, Damon Biotech, and Enzo Biochem) have stockholder equity (operationally defined as the market value of a company's stock minus the long-term liability) in the tens of millions of dollars. In contrast, most of the boutiques are valued at $500,000 to several million dollars. Another indicator of the difference in fiscal health of the boutiques is the current ratio (current assets divided by current liability). For example, Enzo's 1982 current ratio of 46.0, indicating financial health, can be contrasted with Flow General's 1982 current ratio of 2.2. (As a rough rule of thumb, companies with current ratios below 3.0 are considered to be in poor financial shape.)[30]

Perhaps the most successful of the genetic engineering firms is Genentech in California. Founded in 1976, the company had close to 500 employees in 1983. A model of excellent science and business management and judgment, Genentech had a spectacular first issue, fueled strongly by its interferon work. The first interferon gene cloned by Genentech was scaled up and put into clinical trials in a collaborative venture with Hoffmann-La Roche. A similar scheme was used in the

29. An additional finding of the survey also indicates the acceptance of genetic engineering techniques. Asked what kind of instrumentation would have to be acquired by their corporations to bring interferon to market, 18.2 percent of industry representatives answered fermentation equipment. In contrast, none answered large-scale tissue-culture facilities. (The former are required for genetic engineering applications, the latter for classic preparations of interferon.) In addition, 27.3 percent said improved assay systems would be needed, reflecting knowledge of the volume of work involved in developing a commercial product. It should be noted that not all respondents answered all queries, which accounts for the varying sample size.

30. This is the way this indicator is interpreted by E. F. Hutton.

joint development of recombinant human insulin by Genentech and Eli Lilly and Company, in which Genentech provided discovery-phase work (genetic engineering skills) and the older drug house participated in scale-up, preclinical, clinical, and production efforts. Genentech, however, is on the way to becoming a full-service company. Through a limited partnership, it raised close to $60 million in early 1983 to expand production facilities and to conduct clinical trials for interferon-gamma.

Enzo Biochem, a New York company, provides another model of a successful genetic boutique. Enzo's first public offering in 1980 raised $4,115,782 for 775,000 shares. This offering was made at a time when the company's balance sheet showed a net loss of $3,465; its gross revenue for fiscal 1979 was only $133,356. The main attraction of Enzo's prospectus was its plans to develop interferon for clinical use. Yet Enzo's real success has been in the development of biotinized probes, involving a novel method of preparing nucleic acids for use as research tools and eventually as diagnostic tests for clinical laboratories. These products have nothing to do with interferon and were not even mentioned in the 1979 prospectus. Enzo has fared well, and the capital it raised on the hopes of interferon has been used in developing noninterferon products to support corporate growth. Enzo's stockholders' equity of $4,124,051 as of July 1980 rose to $16,100,000 by December 1982.

Unlike Enzo Biochem, Southern Biotech, a Tampa, Florida–based firm, was unsuccessful. In just a year the company's position plummeted from being a potential frontrunner in the race to bring interferon to the market to the point of near bankruptcy. The origins of Southern Biotech's misfortunes are essentially twofold: the reliance on sales of interferon destined for clinical trial use as a source of operating capital, and management problems. Because Southern Biotech was commercially involved in blood collection, the company already had an important resource (blood cells) that was needed to manufacture interferon-alpha. Its decision to produce interferon-alpha by using Cantell's method, in which white blood cells are induced in the laboratory to produce interferon, seemed logical. By 1981 the company had succeeded in producing substantial quantities of interferon-alpha; however, it was unable to obtain FDA approval to use the interferon as an investigational new drug, thereby precluding the product's use in clinical trials. At the same time, genetically engineered interferon-alpha became available, making Southern Biotech's product appear obsolete. The company, moreover, experienced severe personnel and research management problems and miscalculated Wall Street's response to its first public offering of stock. Cash flow difficulties, compounded by an ill-timed repurchase of a major investor's share of stock, led to delays in obtaining crucial pieces of research and development equipment. The collective weight of these problems created an unsalvageable situation, which resulted in the company's filing for reorganization under Chapter Eleven of the federal bankruptcy code in May 1982.[31]

Many genetic boutiques involved in interferon use recombinant-DNA processes and are therefore not vulnerable to the shift in technology that proved detrimental to Southern Biotech. Nevertheless, the new biotechnology industry is characterized by extreme volatility in investor interest as well as in the pace of discovery and innovation, which makes young companies prone to difficulties similar to those of Southern Biotech. According to Victor K. Atkins, Jr., an investment specialist in E. F. Hutton's biotechnology group, more than 95 percent of the biotechnological corporations founded since 1978 will fail because of lack of scientific focus, poor management, or undercapitalization. These problems are not unique to biotechnology (small businesses in other areas— for example, the minicomputer market—may also be subject to these failings). Another difficulty of the genetic boutiques has been that their establishment was technology driven and not market driven, though even market-driven corporations can suffer from these problems.

Public attention to interferon in the late 1970s, due largely to the efforts of Mathilde Krim and the American Cancer Society, permitted the U.S. government to prime the research pump and induce industry to invest in interferon R&D. It also allowed a number of spectacular public issues on Wall Street. In October 1980 Genentech raised $36 million through issuance of 1,100,000 shares of public stock. On the opening day the price of Genentech's stock more than doubled, rising from an initial $35.00 per share to $89.00 and closing at a per share price of $71.25. Cetus raised $108.25 million from 5,224,965 shares offered to the public in March 1980, in the largest initial public offering in the history of the American stock market, prompting Cetus's Peter J. Farley to say, "We caught the timing right." It is not by coincidence that many of the genetic boutiques had first public offerings between 1980 and 1982 (see table 3-5).

Despite the appreciable financial investment in interferon and the flood of publicity surrounding the drug, as yet the future of interferon

---

31. Bankruptcy Act of 1978, sec. 1101, 92 Stat. 2549. Chapter Eleven deals with the business rehabilitative provisions of the act.

as a widely used pharmaceutical is still uncertain. At least two small companies based heavily on interferon are in serious trouble. Key Interferon and its parent, Southern Biotech, have filed under Chapter Eleven, and Biotechnologies, a corporation founded for the purpose of producing interferon, has failed. Several other companies (Cooper Laboratories, Biotech Research Laboratories, and Advanced Biotechnologies) have decided to discontinue interferon research. If interferon proves ultimately to be a lost cause—if it does not cure cancer and is not a good antiviral—it will be disastrous for some genetic boutiques. However, as stated earlier, interferon's success or failure is probably less crucial for the large drug houses. According to John E. Kelsey of Burroughs Wellcome Company's Research Triangle Park facility in North Carolina, the sale of Wellferon has already paid back the company's investment in its development. Moreover, since the biotechnology industry is now sufficiently established, a failure of the "demonstration project" will probably not affect future investment and development of the industry.

### The International Scope of Interferon

The extensive international collaboration in the commercial development of interferon (table 3-7) indicates the global enthusiasm for developing commercial biotechnology. In the January 3, 1983, *IMS Pharmaceutical Marketletter,* fifty-eight corporations in fourteen countries were listed as being actively involved in interferon research and development. Often joint arrangements between companies across borders allow the rapid entry of a company into another nation's pharmaceutical market. International collaborations are not new, and multinational academic and commercial linkings have characterized the interferon field since the substance's discovery. Yet collaborations such as those listed in table 3-7 probably would not have occurred as rapidly without the interferon campaign that was mounted in the United States.

### An Industrial Policy for Interferon?

The interferon experience demonstrates extensive interaction between commercial, not-for-profit, and federal efforts. Technology transfer between these sectors is shown by the examples provided in this chapter. Indeed, the rapid development in the interferon field since 1978 could not have occurred without both federal and corporate investment.

Table 3-7. *International Corporate Collaborations on Interferon*

| U.S.-based company | Foreign-based company |
| --- | --- |
| Biogen | Shionogi Pharmaceutical Company (Japan) |
| Collaborative Research Corporation | Green Cross Corporation (Japan) |
| Flow General (subsidiary of Flow Laboratories) | Sclavo (Italy) and Rentschler-Bioferon (West Germany) |
| Genentech | Toray Industries (Japan), Daiichi Seiyak Company (Japan), and Boehringer-Ingelheim (West Germany) |
| Interferon Sciences | Green Cross Corporation (Japan) |
| G. D. Searle & Company | Meiji Seika Kaisha (Japan) |
| Burroughs Wellcome Company | Sumitomo Chemicals Company (Japan) |
| Hoffmann-La Roche | Takeda Chemical Industries (Japan) |
| Schering-Plough Corporation | Essex-Nippon K. K. (Japan) and Biogen S.A. (Switzerland) |

Sources: *Biotechnology Newswatch,* August 16, 1982, p. 6; company annual reports; and discussions with corporations.

Although, owing to proprietary considerations, it is difficult to quantitatively assess how much industry has invested in interferon, the effort is substantial. Not only has there been commercial development of academic interferon findings, but some corporations, most notably Hoffmann-La Roche, have made their products and data available to academic researchers for basic-science studies.

The early federal investment in interferon provided information exchange coordination, some R&D (such as reference standards), and an early market (government procurement for clinical trials). As the field progressed, the industrial-academic interchange has been facilitated by NIH consensus conferences and personal contacts. In 1983 George J. Galasso, head of NIAID's Development and Applications Branch, was invited to sit in on private sessions at several pharmaceutical houses to learn of their progress on interferon. Such evident desire for cross-communication on the part of industry is especially relevant in the context of current discussions in this country on the desirability of developing a Japanese-style industrial policy. An approach often attributed to the Japanese government in developing targeted industries has in fact been operating unofficially in the interferon field in the United States since 1969. Although beyond the scope of this book, it would be interesting to consider whether there has been an implicit "industrial policy" for interferon in the United States.

*Chapter Four*

# Policy Issues

Four principal policy issues related to the interferon experience that have parallels in the larger biomedical community are discussed in this chapter. These are (1) problems of the changing nature of information exchange and the development of secrecy within the research community, (2) problems of funding fundamental research, (3) problems of adequate scientific personnel and expertise, and (4) problems developing from the rapid rate of technological development and application. Although these issues are common to many areas of scientific research and development, they require particular attention now because the work sites of biomedical research and development are changing and the time required to transfer technology from the basic to the applied laboratory is becoming more compressed.

To understand why such changes underlie contemporary policy issues, it must be recalled that biomedical research and development in the United States from the 1950s through the 1970s typically progressed through three phases—discovery, application, and development—with work in the first phase usually separated by location and in time from work in the other phases.[1] Today, however, the speed at which new information can be translated into commercial product development by using genetic engineering techniques allows the work of all three phases to be done at the same work site.

## Secrecy and Industrial Support of Academic Research

The free exchange of scientific information and changes in the way this information is communicated are fundamental issues that have appeared with the development of commercial biotechnology.

Because of their direct commercial application, findings from the

1. For a description of these phases, see chapter 1.

application and development phases of R&D have often been held secret as proprietary information. The portions of work protected by patent law have, of course, been disclosed as part of the patent petition. But disclosure occurs only after significant time has elapsed (varying from three months to several years or more) following the completion of work, the filing of the patent claim, and the award of the patent. In contrast, phase-one discovery work, especially that done in the academic sector, has been rapidly and openly shared.[2]

Commercial success is measured by quick development and sale of products, so that proprietary claims seem natural when discussing work in phases two and three. In contrast, academic success has traditionally come through peer recognition gained by rapid publication or oral presentation of new results. The discoveries underlying the genetic revolution occurred within academic laboratories. Many academic biologists who were expert in the area quickly saw the commercial potential of their findings. Some became principals in genetic engineering corporations or entered into partnership with pharmaceutical houses and chose the cloning of interferon genes as their first commercial research goal. Because of the short time that elapsed between the phase-one discoveries of genetic engineering and the recognition of the technology's phase-two potential, several professor-entrepreneurs performed the late phase-one and phase-two research in their university laboratories. It was inevitable, therefore, that conflicts of interest concerning information exchange would emerge.

### Decreased Information Exchange

In interviews conducted by the author with scientists who have worked with interferon since the early 1960s and have remained active through the period of interferon gene cloning, questions on the nature of information exchange within the field were explored. Uniformly, each

2. Under the traditional model of biomedical research defined in chapter 1, the disclosure of phase-one work through the medium of publication generally occurred immediately following completion of work. Oral presentations, in open forums prior to publication, established intellectual priority and allowed feedback from one's peers. A twist to this disclosure has occurred with the development of commercial biotechnology. This is the premature or "too-quick" disclosure of work, designed to provide visibility related to stock offerings and public image. In the interferon experience, an example of this was the press conference held by Biogen in January 1980 to announce its cloning of interferon-alpha (see chapter 2).

scientist agreed that there was more collegiality and flow of information in the early 1960s than currently. Equally frequent, however, was the observation that in the 1960s the field was composed of a small group of people groping for solutions in an area considered a fringe science. Another significant factor that was recognized as affecting the nature of competition then was that previously the field was wide open, with more obvious questions to be answered than there were workers. In contrast, by 1982, the fascination with interferon had caught on, and most interferonologists were scrambling to be the first to achieve a few well-defined goals—for example, to produce clinically usable interferon and to identify diseases for which interferon therapy is useful.

The interferonologists interviewed offered two general explanations for the decreased information exchange. First, technical advances in interferon purification in the early 1970s made it possible to study interferon by modern biochemical techniques—thus attracting more scientists to the field and increasing academic competition independent of commercialization.

Second, the intense industrial interest in interferon in the late 1970s had a strong effect, as illustrated by two incidents. In the first instance, one of the scientists interviewed noted that in 1980, while he was on sabbatical leave at the University of Warwick in England, his request for interferon to Wellcome Research Laboratories in England was turned down.[3] The scientist's colleagues at the English drug house, which had provided interferon for research for twenty years, explained that the company was thinking of doing the same work.

The second incident concerns a French interferonologist who was solicited by a British pharmaceutical firm to collaborate on the genetic engineering of a human interferon. Although it has been more than two years since the interferon gene was cloned, results still have not been presented because of a secrecy ban imposed by the drug house. The company decided that proprietary protection was more valuable than patent protection. Meanwhile the scientific information contained in the Frenchman's work has become common, but his efforts go unrecorded in the scientific literature, and he is now hesitant to collaborate with

3. As touched upon in chapter 3, the British pharmaceutical industry made a commitment to interferon long before there was reason to assume that it might have antitumor activity because interferon was viewed as a British "discovery," and the industry did not want interferon to become the modern penicillin. (Although discovered in England, penicillin was developed and commercialized in the United States.)

industry. He recognizes that the contractual agreement that prevented him from exchanging information reflects in part his own naiveté, and he predicts that academic scientists in the 1980s will be more sophisticated in negotiating exactly what will be subject to industrial control—when and if to publish, exchange of information before publication, freedom to alter experimental direction, and exchange of reagents.[4]

### Decreased Exchange of Reagents

Two lawsuits filed in the San Francisco Federal District Court illustrate problems with information exchange in the matter of distribution of research reagents.[5] In 1977 Dr. David Golde, at the University of California at Los Angeles, established a line of cells called KG-1 from a patient's blood cells. Dr. Golde provided the KG-1 cells to Dr. Robert C. Gallo at the National Cancer Institute, whose group observed in passing that KG-1 cells could produce large quantities of interferon-alpha. Neither Golde nor Gallo was primarily interested in interferon, however.

In 1978 production of interferon-alpha by recombinant-DNA technique was still an industrial goal. The plan was to isolate the genetic material containing the blueprint for interferon-alpha, insert it into bacteria, and produce interferon in large quantities. The chief technical obstacle was isolating the interferon gene, and KG-1 cells, which produced a large amount of interferon, were considered useful in overcoming this problem. Hoffmann-La Roche and Genentech had entered into an agreement whereby Genentech would do the genetic engineering and Hoffmann-La Roche would provide biological and drug development expertise. Dr. Sidney Pestka at Hoffmann-La Roche received from Gallo's laboratory a sample of the KG-1 cells. The first interferon-alpha produced by Hoffmann-La Roche–Genentech can trace its experimental origins to a derivative of these KG-1 cells.

In the lawsuits that resulted, David Golde, H. Phillip Koeffler, and the University of California contended that they should share in future

4. The position of academe on these issues may be understood further by examining the compendium of university policies toward industrial relations in "Consulting and Conflict of Interest: A Compendium of the Policies of Almost One Hundred Major Colleges and Universities," *Educational Record*, vol. 61 (Spring 1980), pp. 52–72.

5. *Hoffmann-La Roche, Inc.* v. *Golde*, Civ. No. 80-3601 (N.D. California, filed November 13, 1980).

Hoffmann-La Roche–Genentech profits from interferon-alpha, on the grounds that KG-1 cells were a necessary resource to clone interferon-alpha. These suits soon came to be regarded as a test of ownership rights in the biotechnology area. But their outcome cannot provide legal guidance because Hoffmann-La Roche and the University of California reached an out-of-court settlement, with the pharmaceutical house paying the university an undisclosed sum.[6] Nevertheless, the incident demonstrates the potential legal problems involved in sharing commercially valuable information. Golde said that the cells were given to Gallo with the understanding he would not pass them on, and that Pestka "wrongfully induced" Gallo to give him (Pestka) the cells. Gallo said that he received oral permission to pass them on. Gallo, having been caught in the middle, now says, "I won't send anything out of my lab unless it's 100 percent mine or I have written approval from everyone involved."[7]

Formalizing reagent exchange can at the minimum slow down research, as the following example illustrates. When the race to clone interferon-gamma was won by Genentech in October 1981, the leading challengers, who were working at the Japanese Cancer Research Institute and at New York University (NYU), slowed down their research efforts. Having lost the chance for patent protection and having other experimental priorities, they eventually terminated work on the clone. Nevertheless, because both the Japanese institute and NYU are negotiating with commercial firms who wish to "buy" the clone, the researchers involved are inhibited from distributing it to other scientists, even those disclaiming commercial intentions. While circumstances such as these are easy to understand, the traditional routes of free exchange of materials are nevertheless eroded. Proscriptive stipulations of reagent use can stifle the reagent's creative use or lead to costly litigation. The problems of technology transfer from the academic to the industrial sector may also be exacerbated. Redundancy in research could be another consequence; it may be easier to "rediscover" something than to acquire it from another laboratory.

Several interferonologists interviewed voiced concern not only about the withholding of information but also about the dissemination of incorrect information. One example concerns the genetic cloning of

6. See Barbara J. Culliton, "Drug Firm and UC Settle Interferon Suit," *Science,* vol. 219 (January 28, 1983), p. 372.

7. *Wall Street Journal,* December 3, 1980.

interferon-gamma. Several members of academe explained that they decided not to attempt to clone interferon-gamma on the basis of rumors (later found to be false) that the gene had been cloned. The circulating of such rumors may appear to be trivial and merely an old ploy to gain time. From a commercial standpoint, however, time is not trivial, and from the standpoint of academic scientists such false information may have significant repercussions. Research delays may preclude soliciting the necessary funds to enter the race. Moreover, if the subject has become less fashionable in the interim, the work may never be done.

Does the current discussion of secrecy reflect an irrational fear of the academic community during a period in which new forms of industrial-university ties are developing and traditional government and private foundation support is dwindling? Is the cost to the individual academic scientist of having to clear information with an industrial sponsor an excessive price to pay for long-term and generous commercial support? Is the trade-off for the individual scientist the same as that for the general scientific community and for the public as consumers of science? In response to such questions, all those queried by the author said that secrecy created a less desirable atmosphere in which to work, and all admitted exercising free exchange with certain trusted friends. Some felt that even if secrecy impedes research in academe, it may in the long term be better for the general public because it is the indication of commercial investment. At the same time, it was recognized that there is always some degree of secrecy in highly competitive fields. Robert K. Oldham, director of the NCI's biological response modifiers program, which oversees clinical trials of interferon, feels that "whichever way you get results the quickest is best. . . . If it no longer works to have government funding, grants, and basic research done in the university, if it works better in a pharmaceutical institute research laboratory, that's better. What we want is the end result—better treatments, better biologicals, better biomedical research."

The academic biomedical research community has, for at least the past twenty-five years, provided the science base from which the wanted applications were derived. Whether maintenance of the open atmosphere that prevailed on American university campuses in the 1960s and 1970s is critical to keeping such a science base is only now being tested.

Traditional industrial values are after all, not the same as those of academe. Industry is judged by its balance sheet, not by the number of papers published in the *Proceedings of the National Academy of*

*Sciences.* Commercial support of academic research is a fact of biomedical science in the 1980s. The question is not whether the commercial sector should support work in universities but whether commercial interest will result in the breakdown of an independent science base and whether noncommercial support of university research is needed to prevent such erosion.

In view of the fact that data are not available for analysis, it is hard to measure the extent and effect of decreased information exchange stemming from the current obscuring of industry-academic lines. However, an anecdotal example is enlightening. In a 1980 interview the biologist and Nobel laureate Walter Gilbert said: "Research opens and closes regularly. We're just in a transition from a field of basic research to one with a hard technological base."[8] These transitions tend to blur the distinction between basic and applied research and prompt researchers to question whether their work has commercial application. Gilbert appears to have solved his dilemma. At the time of the interview, he was a professor at Harvard and founding member of Biogen, the Swiss-based bioengineering firm. He has since resigned his professorship to head Biogen full time.

## Funding Fundamental Research: A Public Constituency for Science

Perhaps the most crucial and persistent problem facing the academic biomedical community is how to identify continuous sources of funding for research and training. The interferon experience as described in chapter 2 is a recent illustration of how a publicly vocal constituency can marshal support from the federal, nonprofit, and private sectors. What is the constituency for the support of general biomedical research and what are the prescriptions for its future development?

Theodore M. Cooper, now vice president and scientific director of the Upjohn Company, served as assistant secretary for health at the Department of Health, Education, and Welfare during the period of interferon's popularization (1975–77). He feels that the public constituency for science that was operative then has declined and must be reconstituted if American biomedical science is to retain its eminence.

8. Ibid.

What caused public enthusiasm for the biomedical enterprise to decline?
Cooper believes that

> there has been an erosion of the perception of scientific productivity in this
> country in general and a tarnishing of the scientific image. The tarnished
> image comes from a couple of areas. First, the increased number of reports
> about scientific fraud. Second, some academic scientists are becoming
> entrepreneurs. This is giving groups in the government, legislative, and
> technical [communities] ammunition to say that they won't be mystified by
> the science community.

Does the interferon experience substantiate Cooper's comments?
Although no examples of fraud have been associated with interferon,
the scientific community's failure to dispel the overblown hopes for
interferon may well have contributed to the "tarnishing" of the scientific
image. Regarding Cooper's second point, interferon has certainly been
an obvious example of the development of scientist-entrepreneurs.

Cooper offered several perceptions on how to renew public enthusiasm for science.

> I believe that there needs to be a reconstitution of the constituency of science
> and its leadership. Large sectors of effective political support in Washington
> have never really been mobilized by the scientific research community. They
> have never been asked, to my knowledge, to specifically make it a part of
> their legislative intentions to support science. I don't know that they wouldn't
> do it, but they would benefit greatly from a healthy, vigorous, academic
> science enterprise.

Cooper himself exemplifies what is perceived as a trend in American
medical science, that of the movement of the most highly talented people
from the public to the private sector. This may be attributed to decreasing
support for federally funded university-based research, together with
augmented in-house research within the biotechnology-pharmaceutical
industry. This situation is forcing a reevaluation of industrial-academic-
federal relationships. According to Cooper, "The fact that the values
[of industry and academe] are different is an asset because you're not
deluding yourself about different goals. As far as I'm concerned, industry
couldn't be profitable without a strong academic connection."

### Industrial Support of Academe

Much has been written about whether increased industrial support of
academic biomedical research will alter the nature of the biomedical
academic enterprise. Agreements signed in the past few years between

major universities and industrial sponsors (for example, Hoechst AG–Massachusetts General Hospital, and Monsanto–Washington University) have been the focus of public discussion.[9] Industry is perceived as buying several commodities in these arrangements—for example, a "look-see" at new areas for future commercial development, the right of first refusal on new discoveries, and exclusive consultative agreements with leading scientists. If Cooper is correct that industry will have less need in the future to purchase discovery power as its own R&D effort expands, what will industry require from a healthy academic enterprise? According to Cooper,

> We're becoming less dependent on the discovery mode because we are investing more in our own laboratories, partly because the opportunity exists and partly because we couldn't always get the cooperation that we wanted. When we come to testing the clinical and improved protocols, we need academic institutions. We can't replicate everything in medicine and we haven't got the patients. I don't think that's corruption because it's a straight, open relationship that is done voluntarily. If I give you $5 million and I want the right of first refusal on everything, that is a problem for the university and I don't think it's necessary.[10] I would approach those institutions or departments with a productive environment and just as I'm willing to pay overhead on contracts, I'd be willing to consider paying intellectual overhead in the form of an unrestricted grant to give money over a period of time for libraries, physical plants, training. Such a general research grant helps stabilize [the university] and attracts people, and that makes it attractive to people to stay in academia. I think a company could do that as a programmatic investment, and I would be willing to go to my board of directors and stockholders of the company and try to convince them that that's cheap at twice the price.

Both trained personnel and research that is not immediately commercially relevant will continue to be sought from academe by industry. Though all the industry scientists and administrators interviewed for this study agreed that a healthy academic sector is the basis for productive American industry, not all were as sanguine as Cooper about industry's support for an independent academe. J. Allan Waitz, president of DNAX Research Institute, noted: "I think as long as industry is asked to support research, they're only going to support research that's in their own interest; there's no question about that."

Supporting this view is the experience of Dr. Arthur S. Levine, an

9. See Barbara J. Culliton, "The Hoechst Department at Mass General," *Science*, vol. 216 (June 11, 1982), pp. 1200–03; and Culliton, "Monsanto Gives Washington U. $23.5 Million," *Science* (June 18, 1982), pp. 1295–96.

10. See the discussions in ibid.

NIH oncologist who fears that if basic science research is left solely to industry, the science base will erode. In the fall of 1982 Levine gave a lecture on interferon in the "Medicine and the Layman" series organized by the NCI in Bethesda, Maryland. His fear was confirmed for him by the response to his talk, in which he voiced skepticism about the future use of interferon in cancer therapy. The first row of his audience was occupied by venture capitalists, and at the end of the talk, several approached him with the comment that he had just saved them a great deal of money.

Since the 1950s federal support for academic research has fallen into four categories: training of personnel, specified research, capital expenditure, and physical plant maintenance (in part through indirect cost recovery). Which of these federal roles is likely to be supported in the future by the private sector? Most "genetic engineering" currently done in both academe and industry involves work in phases two and three. Some people are concerned that if university-based research is increasingly supported by private sources, there may be dwindling support for the phase-one work that will underlie the next biomedical revolution. The federal government can ill afford, they say, to decrease substantial support in any of the funding categories if the United States is to maintain a competitive world position in biomedical science.

As is being increasingly demonstrated, however, economic considerations may preclude the government from being the sole source of academic research. Is it feasible to mobilize industrial support for universities in a manner that—to avoid conflict of interest—does not link individual universities or academic workers with an industrial sponsor? One suggestion, as described above in the quotation from Cooper, is that the commercial sector be organized to lobby for federal support of university research. This would use leverage by influential groups, such as American pharmaceutical houses and suppliers to the drug industry, in a way that does not directly affect corporate earnings.

Another example is provided by the Life Sciences Research Foundation, which is a program developed with industry support to provide financial backing for postdoctoral training. The foundation was established in 1981 by Donald D. Brown at the Carnegie Institution in Baltimore. Brown saw a paradox in the simultaneous enthusiasm for commercial biotechnology and the decreasing federal support of fundamental research in terms of the ability to perform independent basic research. A mechanism was sought to entice industry to feed back to academe a portion of biotechnology's proceeds in a way that would not be corporation specific and would not disturb the traditional academic format. With financial support from the Josiah Macy Foundation, Brown assembled a prestigious scientific board and established a not-for-profit organization empowered to collect funds from industry for the purpose of administering postdoctoral fellowships. The fellowships, awarded on a competitive basis, are judged only on the basis of an applicant's qualifications and scientific promise. Individual corporations pledge to provide funds for a circumscribed period of time. However, the foundation makes independent decisions about who receives the fellowship, and provides nonremunerated peer review of applications by prestigious scientists. Although the award that the fellow receives includes the sponsoring firm's name (for example, the Monsanto–Life Sciences Research Foundation Fellowship) and the fellow is encouraged to visit the firm, there is no proprietary access to the fellow's work.

Brown believes that the fellowship process will eventually allow an elite cadre of scientists to be identified, and that prestige (in the public relations sense) will accrue to industrial sponsors as compensation for their investment. In addition, some of these fellows may find their way into industry. One agriculturally oriented sponsor, Pioneer Hi-Bred International, wrote after pledging support:

> I might explain to you the reasons for our decision. First, we intend to devote a certain amount of our research grant money to basic plant science. Second, we wish to encourage those scientists who wish to change their field of research and move into the study of plants. Third, we are interested in having scientists in basic plant research visit companies such as ours in order to become acquainted with [the companies'] scientists, their research potential, and needs. . . . We believe that the two-way educational effects of such meetings can have long-range beneficial effects on basic scientific research in plants. Fourth, we are impressed with the makeup of the board of directors of the Life Sciences Research Foundation and believe that this board will choose genuinely superior individuals as fellows.[11]

The first foundation fellowship awards were announced in March 1983. If Brown's experiment to support the training of excellent young scientists while reeducating industry in how it might support academe is successful, it may prove to be a working model of what Theodore M. Cooper described earlier in the chapter as industrial support of the nation's "intellectual overhead."

· 11. Letter from Donald Duvick, director of the Plant Breeding Division of Pioneer Hi-Bred International, to Donald D. Brown, September 1982.

*Conflicts of Interest*

The debate over industrial support for academic basic science has at its core the possible conflicts of interest between the academic scientist and an industrial sponsor, some of which have already been described here. When commercial considerations arise, there are also conflicts of interest between the government and the university. If work is conducted with federal support, who owns the commercial rights? Should the taxpayer be asked to pay twice, once for the research and again for development? In addition, industry can appropriately ask the government to foster technology transfer. Recent policy changes in the federal patent and trademark laws make it easier for universities and their professors to hold exclusive patent rights.

These changes, in the form of amendments to the public law,[12] accord contractors (for example, a university doing work supported by a government grant or contract) the right to title of inventions made with federal support. (Formerly, the government held the right to such titles and universities had to petition for the right to hold title.) The relevance of this law for technology transfer is clearly stated:

> It is the policy and objective of the Congress to use the patent system to promote the utilization of inventions arising from federally supported research or development; to encourage maximum participation of small business firms in federally supported research and development efforts; to promote collaboration between commercial concerns and nonprofit organizations, including universities; to ensure that inventions made by nonprofit organizations and small business firms are used in a manner to promote free competition and enterprise; to promote the commercialization and public availability of inventions made in the United States by United States industry and labor; to ensure that the Government obtains sufficient rights in federally supported inventions to meet the needs of the Government and protect the public against nonuse or unreasonable use of inventions; and to minimize the costs of administering policies in this area.[13]

In addition to the law's provision that the contractor has the right to elect to hold title to an invention, the law helps ensure that discoveries do not go undeveloped, by requiring that the contractor disclose to the granting agency "within reasonable time" the discovery and whether there is interest in holding title. Should the contractor elect to hold title, attempts to license the invention must be periodically reported. The

12. Patent and Trademark Amendments of 1980, 94 Stat. 3015 (P.L. 96-517, 96 Cong. 2 sess.).

13. Ibid., ch. 38, sec. 200.

intent of this provision is to encourage rapid commercialization of discoveries. As further insurance, the government retains "march-in rights." This law therefore facilitates the ability of universities to benefit from government-supported research.

Conflict-of-interest questions also arise in the current debate over how to support basic science at the NIH. A common theme of the Reagan administration has been to explore means by which roles of the federal government can be transferred to the private sector. It has been suggested that perhaps industry should support the NIH research effort.

The NIH has received private-sector funds for some time and has used them in two ways. Funds have been given, first of all, to the Foundation for Advanced Education in the Sciences (FAES), a private organization that provides services that the government and the NIH are not allowed to do. Examples of FAES services are running a graduate school and offering evening courses with faculty culled from NIH staff, and operating a bookstore on the NIH campus. Funds are also accepted by the NIH into Gift Funds and Patient Welfare Funds. Such contributions are deposited in U.S. Treasury Department accounts, and their use is restricted by law. In some cases these funds can be used for capital expenditures and to pay government employees' salaries. In keeping with Reagan's overall initiatives to diminish the federal role, a committee under the direction of Thomas F. Malone, deputy director of the NIH, has been convened to determine policies that might stimulate the private sector to support work at the NIH using the Gift Funds as a formal mechanism. Problems that need to be addressed are in large part political. Considering that the NIH budget is determined by Congress, if private-sector contributions can be used for capital expenditures and salary, and if such an effort is successful, what will happen to the the NIH's budget? Will Congress be tempted to allow industry dollars to replace federal funds? And what can be said about the continuity of funding for the NIH by the private sector? Can the country afford to allow the funding of a major basic science and clinical research resource to be at the discretion of private-sector contributions? Moreover, if industry is to provide substantial support, it must have appropriate motivation. If the research agenda is not in industry's interest, can motivation exist?

## Manpower: Linking Productive Research and Training

The interferon experience points up several concerns about biomedical research staffing. First are problems of quality staffing of academic institutions. Recruiting and retaining quality faculty are central to maintaining a healthy fundamental science base and to training bioengineers who will staff the commercial sector. (Of the fourteen interferon basic scientists who were extensively interviewed for this study, two left academic positions for industry jobs during the course of the project.)

A second set of problems are short term and are likely to persist for only one or two generations. Currently, there is only one pool of high-quality, mature biotechnology professionals from which to draw, and many of them hold industrial and academic positions simultaneously. For instance, of the twelve just-mentioned interferonologists who remain in academe, six held consultantships related to industrial production of interferon (including scientific directorships on corporate boards) during the period of this work. As future generations of genetic engineers choose between academic and industrial careers, the shortage of mature individuals should decline, assuming the entry of adequate numbers into the profession. The question during this transition period is how to provide sufficient personnel for both sectors without damaging the academic science base. To understand the interrelationships of these staffing issues, the links between research training and competitive research must be examined.

An academic biomedical scientist's work is a team effort done largely by students and postdoctoral trainees. The average time required to receive the doctoral degree is 5.0 years. Of this, 1.5 to 2.5 years are spent in formal course training, and the remaining time represents laboratory research and thesis preparation. The student's training experience cannot be separated from the professor's research product. Therefore, support of research is support of student training, and conversely, funds earmarked for training can be viewed as research support. For example, some medical schools administer medical scientist training programs (MSTP), which are federally funded programs that provide tuition, living stipend, and consumable research supplies for students pursuing joint medical and doctoral degrees. Students with these fellowships are actively sought by faculty research advisers, partly because they rank in the top percentiles of their classes and, not insignificantly, because they bring their own funds. Similarly, the research efforts of postdoctoral trainees are integral to the academic scientist's productivity. In the contemporary environment, persons looking for a research career expect to spend two to four years as "research apprentices" or "post-docs."

Part of the reason for extensive postdoctoral training is that academic research positions are increasingly scarce as faculties decrease in size and become largely tenured. Yet the importance of these "trainees" to the nation's science effort is well known. A panel of the National Research Council studying the national needs for biomedical research personnel cautioned against a dramatic decrease in postdoctoral training funds as a way to bring scientific personnel and jobs into parity.

> The committee recognized that these training funds "make a major contribution to the vigor and quality of American biomedical sciences." The committee was not certain that a reduction in federal training funds would result in a proportional decline in the number of Ph.D. degrees awarded in the future, but was persuaded that a sharp reduction could have a detrimental effect on the quality of the whole enterprise.[14]

As the number of positions in academic research dwindles, trained researchers move to other sectors. One result of the recent technological revolution in biology has been to alter traditional career paths—at least as they relate to the way in which job priorities are set. The comments of Theodore M. Cooper, of the Upjohn Company, reflect this change.

> Current times have some pretty good opportunities for industry. We are in a situation now where we [industry] could hire some people. With the squeeze on the schools, they don't know what to do with their graduates. When I was a graduate student, the ideal first choice for a job was a postdoc at Harvard. Second was NIH. Third, you went to another first-rank university. Fourth, you went to a lesser institution but with a higher faculty rank. Fifth, you went to a government regulatory agency. Last, if you really couldn't get any other job, you went to the pharmaceutical industry. That's what faculty members taught the students. Academia was neglecting one of its major responsibilities, which is to make people for all sectors of society, instead of trying to make everybody a guy at NIH or a professor at Harvard, or even a professor at all. We should have been aware that one of our jobs was to make people who could perform in other areas. Now, we are able to attract some pretty good guys, maybe not for the right reason, but we're not going to argue about that.

Perhaps industry can now benefit from the hard times on campus. However, the goal is to meet both the university's and industry's manpower needs without exacerbating either's problems. Models for generating solutions to some biomedical staffing questions may have parallels in the traditional engineering sciences.

### Future Manpower Issues

Certain parallels exist between the staffing needs of biotechnology and engineering. The American Society for Engineering Education

---

14. Porter E. Coggeshall and others, "Changing Postdoctoral Career Patterns for Biomedical Scientists," *Science*, vol. 202 (November 3, 1978), pp. 487–93.

(ASEE) and the American Association of Engineering Societies (AAES) recently surveyed engineering needs in the academic community. The editors summarized the survey as follows:

> Engineering schools find themselves in the grip of a crisis brought on by too many students and too few faculty, as well as obsolete equipment and facilities. Austere budgets have kept faculty salaries and graduate stipends too low to compete with industry's offers. Federal aid can no longer be relied on, and even massive infusions of industry money, though needed and welcome, go only so far (and, given the troubled economy, perhaps for only so long). The many schools that are not beneficiaries of corporate philanthropy may find the competition for faculty and graduate students just that much harder.[15]

Although there are significant differences between the engineering and biomedical research professions,[16] each of the problems stated above currently exists in biomedicine. In addition, as genetic engineering becomes widely applied in industry, the similarities between training biological engineers and other engineers for private industry converge. Engineering staffing problems and solutions may therefore be studied for their relevance in formulating biomedical research and training policy. John Geils, staff executive of ASEE, stated in a review of the 1981 AAES-ASEE survey:

> The delicate part of the problem is timing; corrections to the engineering education system may take four to seven years to implement, and the economy can turn several handsprings in that period. It is unrealistic to suggest that our engineering education system can be made recession-proof or that we can sever the dependence of our system on the economy. What remains crystal clear, however, is that technology relentlessly continues to become more complex in every way. Engineering is the key to providing new technology and to maintaining and updating that which is in place. We should redouble our efforts to overcome the faculty shortage and [manpower problems].[17]

Three solutions to manpower problems that are currently being tested in engineering are described in the following paragraphs.[18]

15. "Solutions," *Engineering Education,* vol. 73 (November 1982), p. 155.

16. Traditionally, engineering has been a profession requiring only bachelor's or master's degrees, and few Ph.D.s have been sought by the industrial sector. In biomedical research, holders of doctorates who also have postdoctoral training have been the norm. However, as biotechnology flourishes, terminal bachelor's degree and master's degree programs are being developed to meet industrial needs. New biotechnology programs are appearing, such as that at the University of Maryland, College Park.

17. John Geils, "The Faculty Shortage: A Review of the 1981 AAES/ASEE Survey," *Engineering Education,* vol. 73 (November 1982), p. 154.

18. "Solutions," pp. 155–58.

First, to compete with the financial appeal of industry for engineering faculty and to retain superior faculty in academe, it has been suggested that industry provide funds to supplement faculty salaries. Industry's incentive to do this would stem from its long-term stake in high-quality engineering schools, whose graduates may ultimately enter industry. The idea is attractive so long as funds are managed independently of the industrial donor—as in the case of the earlier-mentioned Life Sciences Research Foundation—or provided the recipient university controls the disposition of funds; otherwise, conflict-of-interest problems arise. This solution, if applied to biomedical faculties, would acknowledge that traditional academic rewards alone do not satisfy contemporary biomedical scientists. It should be noted that M.D.s in medical school faculties are traditionally paid more than their Ph.D. colleagues, to compensate for the former's higher perceived market value. This is essentially what is now being suggested for biotechnology professors, but with the innovation that industry contribute to faculty salary support.

Second, to provide continuing education for engineers and engineering faculties and to handle faculty shortages, several engineering corporations have contracted with universities to provide instructors for courses in their company's area of expertise. This is not the same as having a full-time faculty member who is also a principal in a for-profit corporation. The suggestion is feasible, provided such adjunct faculty teach but do not engage in research training at the university. In one model the corporation supplies the instructors and the instructors change each semester. This change in teachers is essential to maintain the separation of corporate and academic identities.

Third, to confront the problems of outdated physical facilities, the engineering community is discussing the possibility of sharing specialized facilities for some training. When such a suggestion is put to the biomedical science community, the question arises of how many centers of excellence are needed. The answer to this question will not be possible until there is a consensus within biomedicine both on the importance of quality research training in educating researchers and on how much "critical mass" (that is, size of the research community) is required to ensure a quality research experience. Once such a consensus is reached, universities might, for example, provide students with some graduate education (for example, formal courses) and then send them to quality academic research centers for their thesis research. This would acknowledge the link between research and training. While all institutions would provide some training, a smaller number would offer practical research training. Some corporations are now allowing students to train in industry laboratories (for example, postdoctoral training positions are offered at Genentech). However, such an arrangement has drawbacks, owing to conflict-of-interest issues and the different research priorities established in university and industry settings.

## Dilemmas Arising from Rapid Technological Change

The new technology will increase two sets of problems: those related to obsolete reagents and those in the regulatory and patent areas.

### Obsolete Reagents

The shortening of the time period between phase-one and phase-three science contributes to the speed at which reagents become obsolete. Several problems arise from the use of obsolete materials in ongoing research. In a recent conversation with the author, DNAX Research Institute president J. Allan Waitz discussed how quickly interferon work can proceed from phase one to phase three.

> [Assuming you have an assay for the protein, first] you have to clone the gene and then figure out how to isolate it. Then you come to the analytical processes and scale-up. Schering now has a facility with 9,000-gallon fermenters in Union, New Jersey, dedicated to making interferon for clinical trials. If you don't have one of those, you've got to build one. If you have one, then you've got a leg up. But the analytical procedures—two-dimensional gels, HPLC [high-pressure liquid chromatography], antiviral assays—in a production setting are different than in a laboratory. If things go well, this is a five- to seven-year process. Once you've done this development for one interferon, you're in good shape. For a second or third interferon you can chop off a couple of years. Then there are toxicology studies (one and one-half to two years) and then three to five years of clinical trials.

One example of the obsolescence of a reagent caused by the rapid introduction of a new interferon occurred in placebo-controlled trials for interferon's prophylactic use in renal transplant patients at the Massachusetts General Hospital in Cambridge, begun in late 1978 under the direction of Dr. Martin S. Hirsch. The interferon used in the study was a Cantell-type preparation of human interferon-alpha, the most potent and the purest interferon available at the time the study started. It was acknowledged that only 0.1 to 1.0 percent of the protein in that preparation was interferon. Furthermore, although the material was derived from pools of mixed patient leukocytes and was prepared according to standard protocols, differences between batches were known to occur. During the course of the trials, recombinant interferon-alpha became available for clinical use. The rapid technological change allowed by genetic engineering techniques made the materials used in the Massachusetts General Hospital trials obsolete. The question arises whether one could or should switch to the new material and whether the trials should be completed. Hirsch noted:

> We didn't start with recombinant interferons because they weren't available when these studies started. I've since been approached by Hoffmann-La Roche to do exactly this study in renal transplant populations using their alpha-interferon preparation. I certainly told them that we'd be interested once the current study is completed. I don't think it would be the wisest course to prematurely terminate an ongoing study or switch from one kind of interferon to another in midstream. I think that with our study more than half completed, before launching a major program it would be useful to have additional data using Cantell's interferon. We would then decide on the basis of our two studies what is the best course, the best dose, the best patients to study, rather than starting still a third study using a different preparation of interferon, but one that isn't all that different biologically, so far as we know. In the meantime, we have begun a different kind of study with the Cantell preparation and we're just going to plug the Hoffmann-La Roche preparation into that and see how they compare.

Because of the length of time required to perform clinical trials, the obsolescence of the reagents being tested may not be unique to biologicals made by genetic engineering. But reagent obsolescence will undoubtedly occur more frequently as new technology is employed. Strategies are needed to determine whether programs should be delayed when products are known to be in the genetic pipeline. Another example illustrates this point. In the fall of 1981 the Lausanne, Switzerland–based company Cytotech invested approximately $150,000 for a New York University–based academic laboratory to develop a method to purify interferon-beta produced by traditional means in cell culture. While this work was in progress, the commercial production of recombinant interferon-beta became feasible. By January 1983 an elegant cell-culture method had been perfected for Cytotech's use, but by that time there was little if any market for nonrecombinant interferon-beta.

The value of information to be gained about a given compound must also be reevaluated in light of the potential for technological obsolescence. What information is worthy of being obtained by using impure material prior to the availability of a purer reagent? With both recombinant and natural interferons available, which should be employed, and should the different interferon preparations be compared in a parallel way? Since patient trials are costly and patient populations limited, escalating numbers of related recombinant reagents create a pressing need to reevaluate how human experimentation is performed. Should the decision rest with the market? Should the companies that can fund clinical trials determine how many variants to evaluate?

From the standpoint of the research community, reagents made by recombinant-DNA techniques conclusively replace older obsolete preparations. Studies that are not "state of the art" (in other words, that do not use the best available materials) fare poorly in terms of grant review and in publication potential. Furthermore, what does reagent obsolescence do to the planning for biological stockpiles? Much of the interferon purchased in 1979 by the NIH remains unused. Ironically, not enough of this interferon was originally available for adequate clinical trials.

An added problem for laboratory research is the discounting of proposed work, based on a perception of how fast results can be achieved by using genetic-engineering techniques. For example, an interferonologist who has been supported by NIH grants for the past ten years was recently denied funding for a grant's renewal. The peer review criticism accompanying the decision indicated that the reviewers did not think that a small laboratory could compete with the pace of progress of larger industrial units, whose findings would rapidly make the scientist's proposed experiments outmoded. This is not an isolated event and has certainly happened in other areas. It shows that the interferon field has reached a level where a critical mass of workers and resources, substantially larger than before, is needed for a laboratory group to be competitive.

. *Regulatory and Patent Problems*

Regulation is another area in which the ease of generating new variants of biologicals brought about by new technology has ramifications. An average interferon protein is composed of 150 amino acids. Once a gene has been cloned, it is simple to alter any of these amino acids, from the standpoints of both scientific difficulty and capital investment. Each variant—even if it differs from another interferon by only one amino acid—is a distinct protein. The potential number of interferons that can be envisioned is easily found by simple factorial calculations.

One aim of current interferon research is to find variants with improved pharmacological characteristics. It has also been suggested that interferons might be custom designed for specific diseases. Under current FDA regulations, each variant is a new drug and must be independently evaluated. Can the regulatory apparatus handle the number of reagents that can be rapidly created using new techniques? Additional regulatory concern focuses on the safety within the work place and in the environment of the processes and the intermediate products generated during the production of biologicals by genetic engineering. Which regulatory agencies have jurisdiction over genetically engineered products: the Food and Drug Administration, the Environmental Protection Agency, the Occupational Safety and Health Administration, or the Consumer Product Safety Commission? Is there appropriate scientific knowledge to know how to evaluate risks associated with genetic engineering and therefore credibly regulate the products of this technology? Should there be a reevaluation of what is required (for example, safety testing and efficacy testing) for new variants of older products? Not only because of the cost of amassing information for FDA approval but also because of the limited patient populations and restricted markets for slightly variant products, it remains unknown which variables will be limiting for genetically engineered drugs.

Problems corresponding to those at the FDA for the possible volume of genetically engineered products can be envisioned for patent claims should patents on genetically engineered proteins be upheld and used. One amusing anecdote from the interferon experience is that the U.S. patent initially issued to Alick Isaacs and Jean Lindenmann for "Production of Viral Interfering Substances" may expire by the time decisions on the pending recombinant interferon patents are made.[19]

19. Alick Isaacs and Jean Lindenmann, U.S. Patent #3,699,222, issued October 17, 1972.

*Chapter Five*

# Lessons of the Interferon Crusade

The issues raised in this chapter concern the future of the American biomedical enterprise and its academic, commercial, and federal sectors. The ultimate goals of this enterprise are to find solutions to biological problems that will result in improved health and quality of life. Though all three sectors subscribe to these goals, their individual agendas differ. The interferon crusade serves to reemphasize the fundamental lesson that those who set the research agenda determine which problems will be answered.

What follow are reflections on the interferon experience. It must be reiterated that although interferon provides the background for the issues examined, it is only a vehicle for discussion. The dynamics of the interferon effort have operated in other areas of research in the past and will operate again in the future.

## Funding Basic Biomedical Research: An Advocacy Process

Who sets the research agenda? The interferon experience illustrates the ability of an organized group of a few politically sophisticated individuals—from the scientific, financial, and legislative communities—to focus resources and thereby affect progress in a particular field. It shows, moreover, that establishing the direction of biomedical research is in large part an advocacy process and that political skill is as important as intellectual merit. The implication of this lesson is that those who are dissatisfied with the direction of current research must learn to be advocates.

Research is a high-risk operation, and when an area is selected for targeting it is because decisionmakers have been convinced that a particular risk should be taken. An advocate's job is to make the case for a particular research direction. A cherished myth among academic scientists is that targeting basic research does not work because one cannot predict where important discoveries will be made. The interferon experience shows, however, that targeting a research area can work.

Interferon was transformed from pseudoscience to state-of-the-art science because of the resources expended on it. The results of the research were twofold. First, basic-science findings uncovered new biological roles for interferon and opened avenues of research of profound significance for immunology. Second, a critical question was answered, though not with the hoped-for answer: it is now known that interferon is not a magic bullet for cancer; the efficacy of its use in any malignancy is still under evaluation.

Most critics of the interferon effort do not deny that there was value in studying interferon. Rather, they contend that an inappropriate share of limited resources was prematurely expended in one area, with the result that potentially more profitable areas of research were overlooked. There is no satisfactory way to assess the validity of this argument, because there is no way to know how funds spent for interferon research would have been otherwise used or what discoveries would have otherwise resulted. The interferon experience repeatedly underlines a nagging and unresolved problem: in the research game, sophisticated advocates have disproportionate discretion in determining the research agenda. Yet if the rules of the game are changed, there is no guarantee that new patterns of influence will be more pluralistic or wise.

## Need for Continuous Research Support

The vitality of the commercial biomedical enterprise and its ultimate clients, the American public, relies on a healthy academic science base of trained personnel who are engaged in making fundamental discoveries. These discoveries can eventually be exploited for product development. Continuity of research is needed to efficiently meet these needs. On-again, off-again funding undermines the quality and productivity of research and training and leads to the demoralization of the academic scientist. The counterargument is, of course, that assured funding leads to passivity and sloppy research.

Policy decisions that determine the amount and distribution of federal funds for basic research reflect changing interpretations in analyzing costs and benefits where the variables include the choice of research areas and which researchers to employ. In the interferon field, as described earlier in the case of a small laboratory—which is unable to compete with larger, industrially based laboratories—one cost is the loss of an excellent scientist who cannot achieve funding. This cost must be compared with the benefits of attention paid to interferon's development by the private sector.

The current exploration of new forms of industrial support for academe, as reviewed in chapter 4, reflects in large part the initial requirement of industry to buy state-of-the-art technology from a small pool of biotechnology experts and an attempt by academics to solve their chronic funding problems. From a public policy perspective, the enthusiasm of the academic community for large sums of industrial money may be shortsighted, because there are fundamental differences between commercial and academic research priorities. The commercial agenda is product oriented, whereas academic goals are often divorced from practical applications. The current convergence of the research goals of many academic and industry scientists as the applications of new technologies are explored may be temporary. And as industry develops an in-house research capability, its eagerness to support university-based work—especially research programs without obvious commercial application—will most likely decline. The responsibility for support of academic science should therefore not be too greatly or too quickly shifted from the federal to the private sector, because long-term industrial support cannot be assured. If government decreases its direct support of research, it lessens its ability to influence the thrust of research and risks the deterioration of the fundamental science base that is a national resource.

While it is imperative to maintain an active and independent basic-science effort in academe, the public benefits from advances only after their commercial development. Effective technology transfer from the academic to the commercial sector must therefore be provided, with the caveat that the mechanisms of achieving technology transfer cannot occur at the expense of limiting candid and uncensored exchange of scientific information within academe.

## A Renewed Public Constituency

A number of persons interviewed for this study feel that continuing support for the biomedical sciences will require renewing a public constituency. To encourage such a revival, the elements underlying public confidence in science must be examined and understood. One element entails the need to involve the public in the policymaking process. To that end, the public must be given the opportunity to participate in a substantive debate about the need for government to support biomedical research and the health targets that are to be selected. Public interest was fundamental to generating support from both the public and private sectors for interferon. One question still debated is whether excessive hype, which "duped" the public, was responsible for public enthusiasm for interferon. Certainly there was interferon hype, and all segments of the community participated—scientists who genuinely believed that they were on the right track and that money solicited at the expense of candor would be wisely used; investors and the public who wanted interferon to be a wonder drug and did not choose to ask whether the claims might be overstated; and those representatives of the media who reported anecdotes with unbridled enthusiasm. One clear lesson of the interferon crusade is that rational biomedical policy cannot be based on hype. But to avoid hype requires, in part, improved scientific literacy. Although a public more literate in science would provide a more skeptical audience, whether a less emotional interferon campaign could have resulted is uncertain.

The interferon crusade was successful because interferon was oversold. Yet the failures of the crusade, in the form of goals that could not be attained and the loss of credibility for the scientific community, deserve serious attention. To stem the erosion of public support for science, two more elements are needed in addition to the need for public involvement. First, the scientific community must do a better job of accurately portraying its work. And second, it must participate more actively in lay science education.

Were the interferonologists wrong not to publicize early their fears about the side effects of interferon and their realistic assessment of interferon's potential as an antitumor drug? This broad question forms part of an even larger one regarding public versus private information. When should the technical community provide information for public and popular discussion about issues on which there is little consensus within the scientific community? When should the public be told that a substance may be harmful? (Regulators face this latter question continually in performing benefit-risk analyses for drugs and environmental pollutants.) There is no easy way to determine when troublesome information should be made public, but it appears inappropriate to trade on unsubstantiated glowing possibilities while suppressing the more gloomy unsubstantiated ones.

## Need for a Common University Policy on Academic Research

Universities remain a vital part of the U.S. science effort. The current trend for support of biomedical science in universities is through expanded industrial funding. At present, each university has its own policies on accepting funds from commercial sources. This plurality creates confusion, especially in terms of encouraging a broad tradition of industry support.

To facilitate industry support, the academic community should develop a uniform definition of what it views as nonnegotiable values (for example, free information exchange; right to publish without censorship). Agreement on guidelines regarding the appropriate role for professors as entrepreneurs (for example, relating to disclosure of funding and consultancy agreements; use of students in commercial projects; percentage of time allowed on corporate boards) should also be developed. If uniformly applied, such guidelines would aid in the establishment of mechanisms for long-term industry support that would provide more security than is the case in the current transient period of new-technology implementation.

Although many groups represent specific segments of the biomedical community, a common voice is needed. An appropriate forum to develop and articulate the consensus might be a policymaking section of a national organization such as the American Association for the Advancement of Science or the Federation of American Societies for Experimental Biology.

## Fostering Technology Transfer from Academe to Industry: Government's Role

New technologies are expensive to implement, and industry will not enter a field that does not show promise of financial return. Incentives allowing the government to share with industry some costs of high-risk research may be beneficial for industry, academe, and government. For example, new tax incentives for industry to invest in academe should be continually explored. If incentives could generate support for work that the university but not the corporation chose to perform, a mechanism might be developed whereby industry invested in research and training that did not have clear commercial directions.

The 1980 amendments to the U.S. patent laws (P.L. 96-517) clarified the rights of universities, nonprofit groups, and small businesses to hold title to tax-supported inventions (see chapter 4). These amendments allow universities to benefit from commercialization of their discoveries. This positive step in fostering technology transfer from academe to industry should be vigorously enforced.

# Epilogue

The interferon crusade against cancer began in the early 1970s. Fueled by enthusiastic press coverage, the crusade peaked in 1980. By 1983 the reality that interferon is not the panacea for cancer had become accepted, as had the realization that it will be a long time before the indisputable efficacy of interferon is established in selected diseases. Similarly, that interferon will not yield immediate, large commercial profits had become clear.

Although enthusiasm for interferon has been rightly tempered, some aspects of the crusade have been tremendous successes. Advances in basic science have elevated interferon from its status as a pseudoscience to that of a prototype for an important group of proteins—the lymphokines—on which the attention of the medical community is now focused. As a demonstration project for implementing new genetic engineering technology in industry, interferon also receives laurels. The interferon story is not finished, and its achievements will most likely continue to surface in the public press over the next few years.

The interferon experience demonstrates that if enormous resources are targeted for a biomedical problem, an information explosion can be generated. Is the political championing of an area like interferon the most productive way or even the only way to mobilize and direct a national scientific effort? This question is difficult to answer because the manner in which the same resources might have been spent and what might have been discovered can only be speculated on. The lessons of raising unrealistic public expectations, as exemplified by the interferon crusade, are here to be learned, but will they be?

Reminiscent of the 1980 interferon press coverage was a headline that appeared in the March 30, 1983, London *Times*. The headline, "A Natural Weapon Against Cancer," accompanied an article reporting on the first cloning of a lymphokine other than interferon, a substance known as interleukin-2. The *Times* article stated that "an important step towards the testing of a natural substance that may have therapeutic value in cancer and other diseases has been taken by Japanese scientists at the Tokyo Cancer Centre [Japanese Cancer Research Institute] and the Ajinomoto Company . . . led by Dr. Tadatsugu Taniguchi.'' Then, on May 9, 1983, the ''CBS Morning News'' reported on a ''new'' cancer drug—lymphokine. And on August 17, 1983, the *New York Times* reported the filing for a first public issue of another biotechnology company, Interleukin-2, Inc.

For interferon watchers, the parallels are unmistakable. The interferon soldiers have regrouped to lead the lymphokine crusade.

*Appendix*

# People Formally Interviewed

*(July 1981–June 1983)*

BASIC SCIENTISTS

Irwin A. Braude, Ph.D. *Meloy Laboratories, Springfield, Virginia*

Derek C. Burke, Ph.D. *University of Warwick, England*

Eduoard De Maeyer, M.D. *Orsay, France*

Jacqueline De Maeyer-Guignard, M.D. *Orsay, France*

Ernesto Falcoff, M.D. *Institut Radium, Paris, France*

Rebecca Falcoff, M.D. *Institut Radium, Paris, France*

Robert M. Friedman, M.D. *Uniformed Services University of the Health Sciences, Bethesda, Maryland*

Ion Gresser, M.D. *Villejuif, France*

Sidney E. Grossberg, M.D. *Medical College of Wisconsin, Milwaukee, Wisconsin*

Ian Kerr, Ph.D. *Imperial Cancer Research Fund, London, England*

Mathilde Krim, Ph.D. *Memorial Sloan-Kettering Institute, New York, New York*

Arthur S. Levine, M.D. *National Cancer Institute, Bethesda, Maryland*

Luc Montagnier *Institut Pasteur, Paris, France*

Jan Vilček, M.D. *New York University, New York, New York*

CLINICAL SCIENTISTS

Jordan Gutterman, M.D. *M. D. Anderson Hospital and Tumor Institute, Houston, Texas*

Martin S. Hirsch, M.D. *Massachusetts General Hospital, Cambridge, Massachusetts*

Thomas C. Merigan, M.D. *Stanford University, Palo Alto, California*

Hans Strander, M.D. *Karolinska Institute, Stockholm, Sweden*

SCIENCE ADMINISTRATORS

George J. Galasso, Ph.D. *National Institute of Allergy and Infectious Diseases, Bethesda, Maryland*

John LaMontagne, Ph.D. *National Institute of Allergy and Infectious Diseases, Bethesda, Maryland*

Cedric Long, Ph.D. *Frederick Cancer Research Center, Frederick, Maryland*

Maureen W. Myers, Ph.D. *National Institute of Allergy and Infectious Diseases, Bethesda, Maryland*

Timothy O'Connor, Ph.D. *Roswell Park Memorial Institute, Buffalo, New York*

Robert K. Oldham, M.D. *Frederick Cancer Research Center, Frederick, Maryland*

Alan S. Rabson, M.D. *National Cancer Institute, Bethesda, Maryland*

Frank J. Rauscher, Jr., Ph.D. *American Cancer Society, New York, New York*

CORPORATE EXECUTIVES

Theodore M. Cooper, M.D. *Upjohn Company, Midland, Michigan*

Peter J. Farley, Ph.D. *Cetus Corporation, Berkeley, California*[1]

Ronald Hoxter *Meloy Laboratories, Springfield, Virginia*

Freidrich Renschler *Renschler Pharmaceuticals, Laupheim, West Germany*

William D. Terry, M.D. *Meloy Laboratories, Springfield, Virginia*

J. F. Von Eichborn *Bioferon, Laupheim, West Germany*

J. Allan Waitz, Ph.D. *DNAX Research Institute, Palo Alto, California*

OTHERS

Victor K. Atkins, Jr. *E. F. Hutton, New York, New York*

Donald D. Brown, Ph.D. *Carnegie Institution, Baltimore, Maryland*

Zsolt Harsanyi, Ph.D. *E. F. Hutton, New York, New York*

1. Interview conducted by Michael Snideman.

# Index

Academic community: and commercialized research, 4, 86–87, 100; government support of, 3, 7, 82, 84, 98; industrial support of, 82–85, 98; and information exchange, 76–81; staffing problems of, 6, 87–92; and technology transfer, 86–87, 101
Acquired immunodeficiency syndrome (AIDS), 31
Advanced Biotechnologies, 73
American Association of Engineering Societies (AAES), 90
American Cancer Society (ACS), 22–24, 25, 27, 72
American Society for Engineering Education (ASEE), 89–90
Armstrong, J. A., 46n
Atkins, Victor K., Jr., 72

Baltimore, David, 6n
Baron, Samuel, 11, 47
Billian, Alphonse, 30
Biogen, 25, 27, 28, 76n
Biological response modifiers program (BRMP), 31, 36n, 51
Biotechnology. See Genetic engineering
Biotech Research Laboratories, 73
Blair, Deeda McCormick, 21
Bristol-Myers Company, 33, 61
Brown, Donald D., 84–85
Burke, Derek C., 17, 58
Burroughs Wellcome Company, 73

Cantell, Kari, 11, 13–14, 17, 19–20, 21, 47
Cape, Ronald E., 61
Carter, Stephen K., 33
Cetus Corporation, 25, 61, 63, 66, 70, 72
Chany, Charles, 11
Clinical trials, 61; of interferon, 15–16, 23, 29, 30–31, 33, 52, 92–93
Cloning, of interferon gene, 25, 27–28, 76n, 79–80, 94–95. See also Genetic engineering
Coggeshall, Porter E., 89n
Commercial sector: and development of interferon, 2, 3, 5–6, 25–28, 58–59, 61, 66, 67, 69, 77; international collaboration in, 73; proprietary claims of, 76–81; relations with academic community, 4, 82–85, 86–87, 91, 98, 100, 101; relations with government, 73–74, 86; staffing problems in, 88–89; types of corporation, 25, 26–27, 61, 66–67, 70–73
Conflict-of-interest issue, 4, 86–87
Controls, historical, 15–16
Cooper Laboratories, 73
Cooper, Theodore M., 81–82, 83, 85, 89
Culliton, Barbara J., 79n, 83n
Cytotech, 93

Damon Biotech, 70
Darlene, Dave, 16n
Davis, Dorland J., 37
Davis, Leon, 24
De Maeyer, Eduoard, 10, 11
De Somer, Pieter, 11, 30
DeVita, Vincent T., Jr., 15, 57n
DNA Sciences, 69
DNA technology. See Genetic engineering
Du Pont de Nemours & Company, 59

Eli Lilly and Company, 4, 6n, 26, 71
Enders, John F., 10, 12
Engineering, and biotechnology, 89–91
Enzo Biochem, 70, 71

Farley, Peter J., 67–68, 72
Federal government: and commercial sector, 73–74, 86; extramural funding for interferon research, 41, 43–45, 46–47, 49, 51–52, 54, 57–58; general biomedical funding, 7, 43–45; intramural interferon research, 36–38, 44–45; support of academic research, 3, 7, 82, 84, 98. See also National Cancer Institute; National Institute of Allergy and Infectious Disease; National Institutes of Health
First International Interferon Congress, 69
Flamant, Robert, 30
Food and Drug Administration (FDA), 6, 68, 69, 71, 95